T0265529

# The
# Future
# is Greater

# The Future is Greater

## Maxine Nwaneri

ONE PLACE. MANY STORIES

HQ
An imprint of HarperCollins*Publishers* Ltd
1 London Bridge Street
London SE1 9GF

www.harpercollins.co.uk

HarperCollins*Publishers*
Macken House, 39/40 Mayor Street Upper,
Dublin 1, D01 C9W8, Ireland

This edition 2024

1
First published in Great Britain by
HQ, an imprint of HarperCollins*Publishers* Ltd 2024

HB ISBN: 978-0-00-854837-7
TPB ISBN: 978-0-00-854838-4

MIX
Paper | Supporting
responsible forestry
FSC
www.fsc.org
FSC™ C007454

This book contains FSC™ certified paper and other controlled
sources to ensure responsible forest management.

For more information visit: www.harpercollins.co.uk/green

This book is set in Minion by Type-it AS, Norway

Printed and Bound in the UK using 100% Renewable Electricity at
CPI Group (UK) Ltd, Croydon, CR0 4YY

I dedicate this book to the loving memory of my grandmother Laura Onubogu (Mama Ye).

I am forever thankful that you saw the future as greater decades ago. It is a privilege to carry your legacy far beyond anywhere you could have asked, dreamt, or imagined, from Obosi, Anambra state, Nigeria.

# Contents

# Prologue:
# A Morning Like No Other

I will never forget the morning of Saturday 10 August 2019 for as long as I live.

As soon as I opened my eyes on waking, I knew something was horribly wrong. I could feel a puddle of sticky liquid in my pyjama bottoms, and to my horror it seemed to be growing. A painful, dread-filled knot formed in my stomach and I froze, too scared to look down. I spent several anxious minutes avoiding the inevitable, hoping this would somehow make it disappear, but when, of course, it didn't, I finally mustered the courage to look. My eyes confirmed what I already knew deep down; I had woken up in a substantial pool of my own blood, and it was spreading rapidly. Courage quickly turned to sheer terror as I wondered, *what in the world is happening to me?*

I looked over at my husband Nnamdi, who was fast asleep. He looked so peaceful, and strong. I called to him to wake him up, hoping that he would be strong for both of us, as usual, and make me feel better. In that moment, that's exactly what I needed. After calling and nudging him several times he finally woke up, confused, and asked sleepily, 'What is it, babe?' I lay there struggling to find the right words before finally managing a whispered, 'Come round and look at this.'

He got up and came over to my side of the bed with a totally puzzled, and still very sleepy, look on his face. I guess he was probably hoping to have a quick look at whatever 'this' was and then he could go back to sleep. Except that when he looked down, to my horror, all the sleepiness and strength drained from his face. He looked petrified, confirming what I already feared – this was really bad! Both of us were in full-blown panic mode now, and Nnamdi started pacing the room while I lay there, too terrified to move, being bombarded by frenzied and random thoughts, such as, *What will happen to our lovely new cream-coloured carpets when I finally stand up, with all this blood down there? We just moved into this nice new house, it will all be ruined.*

I can't remember which one of us finally had the now-obvious idea to call for help, but when we got through to the medical advice line, 111, the operator quickly realised that the problem was a serious one and told us she was going to call an ambulance immediately. As I heard those words, the reality of the situation hit me, and I was overcome with the sense that I was dying.

With those damning words echoing through my mind, I started to feel what I can only describe as a gradual slipping away. The activity in the room seemed to drift further and further from my awareness with each passing moment. I could hear sounds, but I was no longer sure what was happening. My sight took on a strange blur, making it tricky to continue to focus on what was happening around me. I didn't even notice when my husband carried me from the bed to our bathroom, or when the ambulance crew arrived and started asking questions. I had sort of zoned out and was slowly fading away.

They say your life flashes before your eyes when you are dying, and that's exactly what was happening to me. Different scenes, people and memories slowly faded in and out as I felt myself begin to leave the bathroom. The actual view from the cold, white bathtub I was lying in was now all one complete blur. From time to time I would refocus on the faces of the ambulance crew, but I struggled to make sense of what they were saying. They looked concerned, as if they were trying really hard to get through to me, but I had no awareness of what they were saying or what was even going on in that room. I was somehow now in my own separate world, which felt really cold. I also felt a sense of peace as I continued to fade away and make my way towards a light that had now appeared in the distance. As I moved towards it I noticed a strange, conflicting and overwhelming urge to come back to the bathtub and look up to the left. I didn't have the physical strength to do this, as all I wanted to do now was just lie in the bath and fly away to the light, but the feeling persisted, almost whispering – 'Look up to the left.' I finally figured that if I really was dying, then 'up to the left' might as well be the last thing I saw.

It took every ounce of strength I had to lift up my now-really heavy head. As the picture on the left of me came into focus, what felt like a lightning bolt went through me as I suddenly realised that I couldn't possibly die. I had to live! 'Up to the left' was my son, Nnamdi Jr., who was fast asleep in his cot, as well as my daughter, who had come into our room and fallen asleep on our bed. Both kids were totally oblivious to the fact their mother's life was hanging in the balance.

My mind began to race, *I can't die! If I die, what will they do?* I had made the decision to breastfeed my son exclusively, so there was literally nothing for the baby to eat in the house. The realisation hit me that, if I died, it could be the whole day before my husband got done with dealing with his dead wife and made it out to buy a feeding bottle and milk. Even once that was done, he would have to teach Nnamdi Jr. how to drink from a bottle – the baby could starve before all that happened.

And what about my sweet girl, Chiamaka? She had been so attached to me and was looking forward to helping me with the new baby. How would Daddy tell her that her Mummy was dead? *No, I definitely can't die*, I resolved in that moment. No matter what it took, I knew I had to live. I needed to be here to fulfil all of their everyday basic needs, as well as the many other dreams I had for our future as a family.

Once that firm decision was made, what I can only describe as supernatural strength began to flood my body, allowing me to cooperate with the ambulance crew, answer their questions and prepare to do whatever it would take to survive. My mind went from foggy to sharper than ever. I was able to cut through all the chaos to get to crystal clarity on exactly how to respond to their questions so we could figure out what was going on and, more importantly, what needed to happen to save my life.

I shared with the paramedics that I had given birth to my son just twelve days prior, which had been quite an ordeal. Like many mums, before he was born I had had the ideal birth plan in mind – from how I hoped labour would go, right through to us bonding and peacefully feeding for the first hour of his life. It was perfect. I'd had my daughter four years earlier and sort of knew what to expect, so I wasn't as terrified of the delivery process as I had been with her. This time felt different; I felt more confident and prepared.

To say nothing could have prepared me for what *actually* happened at Nnamdi Jr.'s birth would be putting it mildly. Immediately after, the rush of joy and the anticipation at the thought of meeting my new baby boy was replaced with one of terror, as my midwife's smiling face turned deadly serious. Before I could ask what was wrong, alarms were screeching and the room was flooded with emergency team members. My baby was whisked away as a sea of medical professionals began to work on me frantically. There was blood everywhere and I wept as the minutes ticked by, asking questions that nobody seemed to be answering. *Am I dying? Is my son okay? What is happening? Why is no one talking to me?* I kept my gaze fixed on my son across the room as tears rolled down my cheeks, wondering if I would ever get the chance to hold him.

At long last, one of the doctors let out a sigh of relief, and I was informed that I had almost died due to difficulties during the delivery of my placenta, which had caused it to go back up my cervix. They had had to work quickly to bring it back out to ensure I survived the delivery process.

I was so grateful for their quick thinking and successful intervention, and to finally be reunited with my son. It was a terrifying and traumatic experience, and the two of us spent many days in hospital afterwards, when all I wanted was to be at home with my husband and daughter.

When we were eventually allowed to leave the hospital, I felt weak, and as if something was not quite right, but I attributed it to the traumatic experience of my son's delivery and all the blood I had lost in the process. A few days later, though, on that fateful Saturday morning, it was clear my instinct was correct: something was still not quite right.

After listening to my birth experience, the ambulance crew

decided to take me back to the hospital for further investigation and treatment. I told my husband to call my younger sister, who lived fifteen minutes away, to help with looking after our daughter. Without hesitation, my sister Uche and her husband Onuora threw their kids in the car and came over immediately.

My son was on a three-hour feeding schedule, so I asked that he be woken up for one last feed before I left for the hospital. As he was feeding, I was still bleeding heavily. Fighting back tears I wondered whether this might be the last time I fed my beloved baby boy. *What would my family do if I died?* I could feel that now-familiar knot of dread forming in my stomach at the thought, but before I could let fear take over, I caught myself and remembered what had become my mantra for the moment: *I can't die! I have to live for them!* I repeated these words to myself over and over under my breath.

That seemed to give me the strength I needed to finish feeding him and hand him back to my husband. As I did, I looked at the time. It was exactly 10am, so I said to my husband, 'I have no idea where they are taking me, or what we will find when we get there, but you have exactly three hours, until 1pm, to find me so the baby can have his next feed.' He nodded. With that, I left in the ambulance as my sister and her family were pulling up in the car.

The whole way to the hospital, I kept repeating my new mantra to myself: *I can't die. I have to live. God, please help me live. I have to be here for my children.* As I repeated this it gave me a sense of purpose, and seemed to usher in a feeling of peace and strength in spite of the circumstances.

When we arrived at the hospital, emergency investigations began, and the fantastic team quickly realised the issue: during the rush to save my life after my son was born, my placenta had been ruptured. As a result, some pieces of it that should have been delivered were not, and they had begun to form clots, which were causing me to haemorrhage. They calculated that I had lost around three litres of blood in total since I gave birth. I didn't think too much of it until I later found out that the body only has around six litres! I was told that it was a miracle I even woke up that morning, as the blood loss I'd experienced could have caused me to die in my sleep. With a clearer understanding of the issue, the team rushed me into emergency surgery to remove the remaining placenta and stop the bleeding. I will be forever grateful to the incredible team working at the hospital – they saved my life twice in as many weeks.

As they wheeled me out of surgery, saying everything should be fine, I couldn't hold back the tears of joy I felt when I saw my husband and son waiting for me in the recovery room. I looked up at the clock above my designated bed – it was almost 1pm. My husband had managed to sort everything out and find me, and I had made it back to them with five minutes to spare before my son's next feed. Nnamdi even confirmed the carpet at the house was fine – one of the first things I asked him!

Tears of joy and gratitude continued to flow throughout the feed, as well as during the life-giving blood transfusions, and on the long road to recovery that followed.

# Introduction

## The power of purpose

In spite of all the trauma, my heart is filled with gratitude when I think back to that day I nearly died – gratitude for my family, as well as for so many others who gathered round to save and support me. I was also grateful for the incredible life lesson that was reinforced for me through the experience; I had rediscovered just how empowering and destiny-altering a sense of purpose can be when we are facing life's challenges.

I believe that connecting to the simple purpose of needing to be a food source for my son and to be there for my family in general is a huge part of why I survived. Connecting to that purpose brought calm, clarity and courage to one of the most terrifying and chaotic situations I have ever faced, and it literally changed everything for me. I am also convinced that is the case for all of us, no matter what we are facing. When we discover our true purpose in any given moment, and begin to move towards it, we unlock strength, resilience, resources and whatever else is needed to overcome even the most challenging circumstances in life. I have continued to be led by a powerful sense of purpose ever since that day.

## Why I wrote this book

It was in that quest to live a life aligned to my purpose that I felt a calling to write this book – one that I hope will help women navigate motherhood in a more empowered way and, quite frankly, give them the opportunity to have it all.

I used to hate the phrase 'have it all' when used in relation to working mums and their careers, as it always brought up visions of some unattainable perfection and sense of balance that we must try to reach. Over time, though, my experience has shown me that we *can* have it all when we take the time to figure out what 'all' means for us as individuals in each season of our lives. Through my life and work, I have found that 'all' can look very different from one woman to the next because, although we may face many similar challenges as women, we are all wonderfully unique. I have also found that having it all can look very different throughout our lives – what a woman may want in her thirties may not look at all like what she wants in her forties, and so on. Whatever a woman's current definition of 'all' is, there are few things more satisfying to me than helping her go from a place of thinking or worrying that it is something that is not possible to achieve, to one where she is living in a reality far better than the 'all' she envisioned.

I believe that we women can have the career, the family, the body, the life – all the things that are meant for us in each season of our lives, even in this age of endless demands and time con-straints. That's my goal with this book; to help as many women as possible go from barely surviving – or whatever point they find themselves – to thriving. I appreciate this might sound like a totally ridiculous and impossible dream to you, especially given how hard things have been for women for literally centuries. So often, we are told, or even expected, to sacrifice our desires for the sake of our families and others, yet I believe in and live by the motto that anything is possible. I've seen the impossible become possible too many times to be convinced otherwise. Creating the impossible had become the norm for me in the over two decades that I'd spent building a successful international corporate career, then launching an executive coaching and leadership advisory practice in which I help professional women create and live out their best possible lives. It's now my job to help women create lives and careers that blow their minds, and if I say so myself, I'm pretty amazing at it! There have been so many surreal moments when my clients have compared their results from our coaching to where they were when they started, and they are completely stunned. I have seen this enough to know, without a shadow of a doubt, that with the right guidance and following a few specific steps, every mother can design her life so she can have it all, no matter where she is starting from.

That said, in all honesty, when I first sensed the call to write this book I felt more than a little overwhelmed and wanted nothing to do with it. I thought, *I'm here struggling with juggling motherhood and a career myself, how in the world am I going to find time to write a book?* So I ignored the urge. But as is often the case with purpose, it just wouldn't quit; sort of like the voice urging me to 'look up to the left' that morning I almost died. I kept procrastinating and putting off the book idea, telling myself that I'd get to it when I had more time and energy, but everywhere I went, I noticed the plight of women, especially mothers, trying to keep their heads above water in the sea of endless demands from work, family, themselves and elsewhere, and my heart broke regularly.

It broke for the mum who is so mentally and physically exhausted but who must find a way to keep going; for the mum who cried herself to sleep last night due to how hard things are but who is moved by love to get up and do it all again today. For the mum who can't find a moment for herself because of all the time she devotes to others. For the one who has lost all sense of who she even is anymore outside of all her responsibilities. For all the mums trying their best and still feeling like it's not good enough, and that they are failing everywhere. My heart broke repeatedly for all of us, and then I felt that bolt of purpose shoot through me once more, and this time it convinced me that I had to write this book – for the sake of all those mums.

## How to get the most out of this book

As you read, I would suggest having a journal or similar to hand where you can make a note of any questions, ideas, thoughts, 'a-ha' moments or anything else that may come to you. I also highly recommend that you do the exercises and implement the suggestions I have included rather than just read them – this will bring the strategies to life and help you to transform your specific situation. I also encourage you to maintain an open mind as you work through these chapters, even if you have heard some of the concepts before, or if the suggestions seem different to anything else you've heard.

Finally, it's worth noting that some of the concepts I share may be more or less relevant to you depending on your current circumstances. I'd love for you to be aware of all of them as you read through initially, then you are welcome to treat this as a handbook that you can come back to as you encounter situations where the tools and practical tips become more relevant and beneficial for you.

## The real reasons why so many of us don't have it all

Once I made the firm decision to write this book, I thought my biggest issue in getting started was finding the time to write. Like most other mums I know, it already felt like twenty-four hours a day was nowhere near enough time to do what was necessary to survive, never mind to achieve grand dreams like writing a book.

When I returned to work after having my second baby I was still navigating significant health challenges and the numerous and time-consuming medical appointments linked to them. Each day felt like a non-stop blur of activities from the moment I woke up until my exhausted head hit the pillow at night. I had no idea how or when I would write this book, but I knew that this was my purpose right now, and a big part of the 'all' I knew I needed to have. Thankfully, my near-death experience after the birth of my son and other life events have taught me that when I am being driven by purpose in this way, I can tap into powerful wisdom from within me to make the most of whatever I have. I am able to at least start moving in the right direction. So that's what I resolved to do. All I had was small pockets of time – ten or fifteen minutes here and there each day – so I started with that. I used those precious moments to tune in to my internal wisdom for guidance regularly, and to learn, research and analyse over two decades of successes and failures from my own life and my work coaching hundreds of women. I had two main goals: first, to figure out how I could better manage my time so I could have more of it to write. The second was to work out how to record all the things that I'd discovered through my experiences to be most conducive in helping us mums manage our time better to achieve our dreams of having it all.

For years, I had heard myself and other working mums say that the main reason we can't have it all is because there simply isn't enough time. Some of us have even joked that it would be great if we didn't need to sleep, so we could use those few night-time hours to finally get our never-ending to-do lists under control. With each child we add to our families, the reality for most us is that it is necessary to make major time-intensive adjustments that impact our career and other goals. We have to take time out from work to welcome our children into our lives, either through their physical delivery, or by other means when we are not the one physically giving birth. Then we need to make sure they are fed and looked after; all of which can take a significant amount of time. If we choose to breastfeed, that in itself can be massively time consuming. Then, when we get back to work, with all the additional responsibilities from our growing family and everywhere else, we have a lot less time. Something has to give, and for most mums – including me – it's usually us, and what we want for ourselves. 'Having it all' begins to feel and sound like some unrealistic, almost laughable dream. We tell ourselves we can't possibly do what we want for ourselves when there are all these other things to do; there's simply not enough time. So we push ourselves and what we want just for us lower and lower down our to-do lists, until eventually so many of those personal dreams die.

Allowing the dream of writing this book to die was definitely not an option for me, so I continued with my work, using those precious pockets of time as best as I could. The more I did my research and considered the predicament of us working mums, the clearer it became to me that this was one of the reasons why I had escaped death that morning: to fulfil the purpose of writing this.

As I worked, I began to question whether I had actually identified the main problem that this book is meant to solve for us mums. My mind was convinced that the primary issue to tackle was the fact that we don't have enough time; however, my gut was not. I had a niggling feeling that there was more to it than that, which led me to scan back over two decades of personal and professional experiences filled with incredible highs and catastrophic lows, to consider this hypothesis. I was genuinely shocked to see that the amount of time I had available had very little to do with whether or not I achieved even the biggest, most impossible-looking dreams in the past. There were many instances when I achieved things that should have taken much longer in a fraction of the time. There were also situations where I had ample time but was somehow still hindered from reaching my goals. So if the amount of time wasn't the issue, what was?

I began tracking what typically happened in the lead-up to situations in the past where I either reached my goals or didn't. I was keen to see whether there were any patterns or clues. As I looked back, over and over again it was clear that my experience of either achieving or failing to reach my goals in any present moment was easily predictable based on the way in which I had used, or failed to use, my time effectively.

As I analysed all this, it occurred to me that the way we use the time available to us is very similar to how we approach our finances; if you make the right investments today, you will make more money in the future. However, if you spend and waste all that you have now, it's more likely that you will find yourself lacking what you need in the future.

The parallels were so clear as I looked back over my life; I could trace the instances when I was able to accelerate towards my goals back to time that was well invested prior to that. Similarly, those moments when I missed out on what I wanted clearly pointed back to poor uses of time in the past, in which I had wasted or mindlessly spent it. As I pondered how all of this was even relevant to working mums I was led one step further, to ask why? Why would we, as smart mums who want to have it all, ever waste or mindlessly spend our time? What was driving this contradictory behaviour?

As I considered specific examples in my life and why I had found myself in time-starved predicaments in those moments, the answer became crystal clear to me: our experiences with time are simply symptoms of other underlying issues. For example, my tendency to want to please others often made me say yes to their requests, even when I really wanted to say no. The issue was my reluctance to muster up the courage to set expectations and boundaries with others and invest time in doing so, which subsequently led to me taking on too much and ultimately depriving myself of spare time.

Another example I uncovered was the fact that I had never invested proper time in creating a true partnership with my husband through which we would tackle the unpaid work at home, even though we are a dual-career couple. This meant that I resentfully did almost everything around the house and, once again – you guessed it – the consequence was the same: not having enough time.

I found powerful insights that aligned with this realisation, even with the process of trying to find the time to write this book or to do other things for myself. My tendency to prefer waiting until that 'perfect' and elusive moment when I would have more time, knowledge, support or whatever it was that I felt I needed, actually robbed me of so much. Underestimating how much can be achieved with whatever I have had available, even if it looks small, led to me not always taking advantage of what I had. I was, in effect, wasting time kidding myself that I'd get to something when whatever stars I was waiting on aligned. Needless to say, they rarely did, so I never did have enough time for what I really wanted to do.

On and on it went throughout my life, and as I traced my over-whelmed schedule and lack of time back to the root causes, I always discovered more deep-rooted issues at work. These issues, though quite different in nature, all had the same devastating impact: they caused me to either waste or mindlessly spend my time, and threatened to kill my dream of having it all. I therefore started calling these issues 'dream killers'. I spoke to hundreds of women while I researched this book, in addition to reviewing my notes from coaching hundreds of others from all around the world, and I noticed the same eight culprits popping up and robbing us of time and so much more:

1. The 'I'll do it when...' mindset
2. Needing to see it to believe it
3. Life crises
4. The curses of comparison and people-pleasing
5. Not putting on your own oxygen mask first
6. Not feeling good enough
7. Life just isn't fair
8. Guilt and overwhelm

Letting these dream killers go unnoticed and unaddressed at different points in my life left very little time for myself, and preventing me working towards those goals that made me feel alive and as if I was fulfilling my purpose and potential. So, let's go through these dream killers one by one and see the impact they have on our lives.

## Dream killer 1: The 'I'll do it when...' mindset

So many of us never even get started on the path to realising our goals and creating our best possible lives because of the 'I'll do it when...' mindset. This first dream killer works by keeping us focused on all the things we lack, which must be taken care of before we can do what we really want to do. God knows that, for us mums, there is always something that we feel we are lacking – and whether that's time, that our home isn't quite how we want it yet, the project at work that needs to be completed, or things that are happening with our kids, there always seems to be something to do first. If we wait for that elusive opportune moment when we'll finally have those things that we feel that we're lacking, we use up all our time and energy focused on other people's urgent and important needs rather than prioritising our own goals. As we push ourselves and our personal goals further down the to-do list, or scale down our ambitions, we tell ourselves that we'll get to them soon, but the reality is that we never do, and our dreams eventually fade.

## Dream killer 2: Needing to see it to believe it

If and when we do get started on those goals that are truly important to us and our purpose, many of us then have to contend with the need to see it to believe it. This dream killer is exemplified by popular phrases like 'we can't be what we can't see', and 'seeing is believing'. While there is some truth to these phrases, they can cause us to start looking for evidence that our dream of having it all is even possible. Unfortunately, this search leads too few women to find the role models they seek, as there are simply not enough of them. Instead, countless mums end up finding a perfect storm of circumstances that seem to directly oppose us and suggest that it's impossible to get what we want in our workplace structures, our societies, or even our homes. Therefore we subconsciously take on the belief that it's not possible to get what we want.

Such beliefs lead us to question whether we have to choose between some aspect of life and another; for example, between a thriving career or prioritising our family. Thoughts entertained long enough lead to action, and we see this played out in the vast numbers of mums all over the world who are reluctantly scaling back and exiting their careers – careers they would have preferred to keep progressing in – because they can't see how it would be possible to balance their work life with the thriving personal and family life that they also want. And just like that, the dream of having it all dies.

## Dream killer 3: Life crises

For those who do manage to keep progressing with their dreams, it is inevitable that at some point they will encounter the next dream killer: the crises that life can throw our way. We all eventually have to deal with things that we never saw coming, which can completely knock the wind out of our sails and send us off track. This dream killer is incredibly effective at totally derailing us from making progress towards our goals, as our default reaction is to immediately devote a considerable amount, if not all, of our time to 'firefighting' and reacting. The result is that we are left with little or no time to focus on anything else, and thus our dreams of anything other than survival inevitably die.

## Dream killer 4: The curses of comparison and people-pleasing

The next dream killer that most of us have to deal with at some point is what I call the curse of comparison and people-pleasing. This can crop up during our interactions with others and can rob us of considerable amounts of time if we don't handle it correctly. For instance, take the other mums in our friendship circle who make us feel like we are not good enough – whether that's through the things they say, they do, or even what they post on social media. When we compare our lives, wishes and expectations to those of others, we may come up short, feel 'less than' or be tempted to give up. Sadly, many mums *do* give up, because they carry the weight of others' expectations on their shoulders and subconsciously design their lives accordingly. These are typically lives in which their own dreams are long gone, and in which they are deeply unfulfilled.

## Dream killer 5: Not putting on your own oxygen mask first

Perhaps one of the most effective and sneaky dream killers of them all is the tendency that so many of us mums have of not putting on our own oxygen masks before we help others. The consequence of this is that we sacrifice our own self-care in the name of caring for our children and others. On the surface, it seems selfless and honourable to put ourselves last after taking care of everything and everyone else first, but in actual fact this is one of the most devastating dream killers in terms of how it can rob us of time, our lives, and even our destinies.

## Dream killer 6: Not feeling good enough

The destruction caused by a lack of self-care is highly conducive to enabling the next dream killer: not feeling good enough. This one often manifests as that fierce invisible critic in our heads; the one that endlessly reminds us of all the things we haven't done perfectly, while at the same time ignoring or minimising all the things that we have done well. The voice that keeps telling us that we aren't good enough, that all our successes so far have been flukes, and that it's only a matter of time before we are found out. On and on it goes, accusing and criticising us, sapping our confidence as we try to reach for our goals, inevitably robbing us of time and efficiency in reaching said goals, leading so many of us mums to sadly give up on our dreams and too many goals in one sentence!

## Dream killer 7: Life just isn't fair

As if that wasn't bad enough, this internal enemy often gets help from external enemies to rob us of more time and fulfilment in life. Almost every woman I have worked with and spoken to has encountered the dream killer of situations that are totally unfair. For example, the fact that so many things in life, work and society are simply not conducive to gender equality, and that people can – either through unconscious or overt bias – discriminate against us in a way that impacts our ability to achieve our dreams. I have lost count of the number of women who have told me that people at work assumed they would not be interested in or able to take advantage of new opportunities because they are a mum, all without ever asking them. These were often opportunities that they *did* want, and that they could have figured out how to make work had others' bias not robbed them of the option. When we experience infuriating and unfair situations like this as mums, if we don't respond in an intentional and empowered way, and instead simply react in a default manner, we are almost guaranteed to waste our time, while also unintentionally assisting the unfair situation in killing our dreams.

## Dream killer 8: Guilt and overwhelm

Finally, there is the mother of all dream killers for mums – guilt, and the overwhelm that often accompanies it. It's so widespread among mums that we even have a name for it: Mum guilt. It's that awful feeling we often have to contend with when we have over-whelming schedules that create conflicting priorities and necessary compromises. So many of us make a choice then feel guilty and worry we have made the wrong one, which will negatively impact us or our kids somehow. For example, we worry we will be viewed as a bad mum, or that it will somehow affect our kids if we choose work when faced with a trade-off between professional and personal priorities. Then if we choose the personal thing – such as attending something at our kids' school – when we have a conflict at work, we worry what impact that will have on us professionally, and how people will view us. These feelings of guilt and worry rob us of so much, both long before and well after the decision or trade-off has been made.

If you have been struggling with all the juggling you have to do in working motherhood, feeling sceptical about whether you can ever have it all, it's no wonder when you consider just that brief summary of the effects of these dream killers in our lives! Please also know that it is definitely not your fault if you have been struggling; collectively, these dream killers have been robbing us blind as women, and causing us to pay hefty penalties in work and life.

In my work with mums over the years, many discussions have come up about the 'motherhood penalty', where women's career contributions and compensations suffer after they become mothers. Contrast that to the experience of men, whom research finds typically enjoy a 'fatherhood premium' of increased compensation when they become parents. This infuriates me, and has added fuel to the fire of my purpose in helping us mums through this book. It's no wonder we have a gender pay gap that feels impossible to close with these penalties and premiums! I suspect that with these dream killers left unchecked it would actually be impossible to ever close the pay gap.

Having invested tens of thousands of pounds on my formal education, and also been well taught by the school of life that anything is possible, I was not about to settle for us having to keep paying this motherhood penalty without a fight. I was determined to tackle these dream killers not just for me, but also for other mothers, and especially for my daughter, to ensure that she does not have to live, work and raise her family in a world where we keep talking about a gender pay gap that will take over a century to close. So I resolved that there was no better time than now to adapt the principles I had been coaching women on successfully for years into a book that would help even more women to tackle these dream killers, so we can finally live stress-free and fulfilled lives.

## How this book will benefit you

I have no idea what specifically led you to pick up this book, but I'm so glad you did. Only *you* know the details of your own journey – the challenges, frustrations, setbacks and all those other things that may have brought you to a place of thinking, *How can this be my life?*, or *This is not what I hoped for growing up'* like so many of the women I have spoken to over the years. With so many demands on your time, and so many circumstances out of your control, you would be forgiven for wondering whether someone writing a book for mums about 'having it all' is in their right mind, or even on this planet. Is it really possible to navigate motherhood in an empowered, fulfilling and successful way as a good mum who also reaches her own purpose-aligned goals? It is especially easy to find yourself wondering this given how much the world has changed.

If you're wondering about any of that, trust me, I get it. I have as well at times, and I've heard it from enough women over the years, too. However, if my life story has taught me anything, it is to never settle for anything less than the biggest dream I have for myself, my family and my life just because of to a perceived lack of time or anything else. I have found everything can be overcome when we align to our purpose and tap into the powerful wisdom within that leads us to the right guidance and steps. As you read these words you may be thinking, *but you don't know my situation, Maxine, how hard things are for me, the lack of support in my life; the people deliberately coming against me.* You're right, I don't, and while my heart goes out to you for every challenge you face, every tear you've cried, and everything that makes you want to give up on your dreams, I still say this: please don't ever settle for living anything less than your best, blow-your-mind kind of life.

Whatever life you believe you have to settle for is not who you are meant to be. You are meant for so much more, even if you can't see how right now. I certainly didn't see any possibilities while I lay in my bathtub with blood, strength and life draining from my body. If I had given in to the dream killer of the 'I'll do it when...' mindset, which would have had me waiting for when I could see possibilities or when I had more strength, there is no doubt in my mind that I would have died that day. The strategy of listening to my inner guidance and connecting to purpose in that moment saved my life, and it led to me writing this book that I hope and believe will save yours. At the very least, it will save you from living anything less than the best life I know you can create and step into, no matter what the circumstances around you might suggest right now.

I have developed highly effective strategies to help you tackle each of these eight dream killers efficiently in empowering ways that will get you on track and keep you on your journey towards achieving your own goals, while still also being able to take amazing care of everything and everyone else you need to. These strategies will help you make simple adjustments that will make a world of difference to you and your family.

I am by no means suggesting that the eight dream killers above are an exhaustive list of every issue you will face as a mother seeking to thrive and reach your goals, but what I am saying is that if you focus on and tackle those issues that are applicable to you by following what I outline in this book, you are likely to accelerate towards a life more incredible than you could have dreamed of.

I believe our wildest dreams can, and do, come true, no matter how bad things are right now. I can say that with complete confidence because I am living proof of this – not just based on my near-death experience, but because of other defining moments and experiences from my life and work that helped me discover the dream killers, and the powerful strategies to overcome them. Prepare to be blown away and have your life transformed!

## The rest of your journey through this book

In this book I will tackle each dream killer in turn, chapter by chapter, starting with the 'I'll do it when...' mindset. In each chapter I will share my own personal journey in discovering each of the dream killers; how they impacted my life, and what I learnt. We will explore how each dream killer can cause us to waste or mind-lessly spend our time as mothers. I will also provide you with the strategies, tips, tools and techniques to work towards tackling the dream killer in your own life by instead investing time to implement the right strategies that will help you overcome it. As is the case with great financial investments, these powerful time investments will deliver you huge returns. Expect to see lots of time being freed up for you to create and live a life in which you consistently accomplish results that previously would have seemed impossible; a life in which you are achieving your goals in work and life, getting adequate rest, practising self-care and finding time to do whatever else your soul craves while also taking great care of your family. No more settling for less than the life you know deep down that you are meant for.

As I looked back over my experiences and those of the clients around the world that I have been privileged to work with, it amazed me to see the massive difference these strategies have made in our lives. We have gone from feeling like we have to put ourselves last and sacrifice our own personal goals and dreams for the sake of family, to being able to navigate motherhood in a way that enables us to thrive and fulfil our own potential while doing our best to raise our families. So many of us feel like we have finally 'got that girl back', as we reconnected with that amazing version of ourselves that somehow got lost with all the mothering.

If it has worked for us, it can work for you too. My hope is that as you read you will be inspired to feel that anything is possible for you, and that you'll be encouraged to use the simple steps and tools to create the future that you are meant for; for you, your family and your life! Wherever you are on your journey, however different your dreams and goals may be to my own, I'm pretty confident that I can help you achieve them.

# Chapter 1: The 'I'll do it when...' Mindset

How many times have you thought of something you want to do for yourself and decided you'd do it when you get to some more opportune moment, like maybe when you have more time? Of all those things you said you'd do later, what percentage of them have you actually ever got around to doing?

If you are anything like most of the women I have worked with and spoken to during my work as a coach, and while conducting research calls for this book, that percentage is pretty low. To be clear, I'm not sitting here on some high horse judging you or any other woman for this; I can totally relate to it myself, as I mentionned earlier, I almost didn't even write this book because I felt I didn't have enough time.

Whether we want to finally have that 'me time' we have been craving, or to start that project in the house, so many of us mums fall prey to the 'I'll do it when...' mindset. We often have to deal with all sorts of urgent and important things for other people that distract us from going for our own goals. As we busy ourselves looking after everything and everyone else, and fighting the fires in life that pop up unexpectedly, there can be a tendency to keep saying things to ourselves like:

I'll do what I want to for myself when…

- I have more time
- I have more money
- I have more motivation
- I have more connections
- I finish this urgent work project
- My kids get to a certain age
- I get more childcare sorted
- I have more answers
- I feel more confident
- I reach that next level in my career
- I have a better idea of how it will work out
- I know exactly what to do
- I can get it done as close to perfectly as possible

These are just some examples, but there may be others that better relate to you and your specific situation. Feel free to fill in whatever it is you've been telling yourself is the right time to focus on your goals and what you really want for you.

## How this dream killer causes us to waste time

The 'I'll do it when…' mindset is an extremely subtle yet effective dream killer because it keeps us focused on all the things that we lack and must have in place before we can focus on us and our own goals. The sad truth is that it's highly unlikely that everything will ever fall so perfectly into place that we can finally do what we want for ourselves.

Is it just me, or have you noticed that there is almost always something else to do that keeps pushing us and our personal ambitions lower and lower down the to-do list? And all the while time keeps ticking on. The days turn to weeks, months and then years where we have spent, and on occasion even wasted, time focused on what we don't have, while attending to everyone else's needs, goals and agendas. Needless to say, we therefore make very little progress towards the life that we would love to be living for us personally, and sacrifice much of what we would have loved to experience both in and out of work.

If you are anything like me and some of the clients that I have worked with, when this happens resentment sets in, then guilt for even feeling that way towards people you love joins the pity party, and so we overcompensate and continue all the self-sacrificing. This once again leaves us with not enough time for ourselves, continuing the sad cycle. There is a better way.

## Overcoming Dream Killer 1: The 'I'll do it when...' Mindset

There are many reasons why women fall prey to the 'I'll do it when...' mindset. It's not my intention to attempt to provide an exhaustive list of solutions to them all, but I would like to introduce you to some simple yet powerful techniques you can use to begin to overcome this dream killer, however it shows up for you.

So when you have something that you want to do and you notice yourself thinking about what you need that you don't have right now, resolve not to give in to this time-thieving, unfocused mindset. Instead, switch your focus from what you don't have to whatever it is you do have, however small it is, and begin to work with it in an intentional manner.

For me, during the process of writing this book, that looked like switching from thinking, *I'll write a book when I have time* to assessing how much time I actually did have to spare. It was barely thirty minutes a day, which felt like such a minuscule amount of time to work with to complete such a massive task, but it was all I could find, so I started with that. To my utter surprise, it proved to be enough to get the job done. The simple time investment of around three minutes to switch my focus and figure out what I did have to work with stopped me from being robbed of thirty minutes a day, which, let's face it, knowing myself would have just disappeared into thin air and remained unaccounted for forever. More importantly, that tiny investment of time prevented me from being robbed of fulfilling my purpose of getting this potentially life-changing book into your hands. Do you see how potent this can be?

Just in case you're wondering what if you have nothing at all to work with, please bear with me. Perhaps you genuinely can't find five minutes, never mind thirty minutes, or even a tiny bit of whatever it is you need. I can certainly relate to this too. There have been so many instances where I honestly could not find the strength, time, motivation or whatever else I felt I needed. In such situations, rather than just allowing the 'I'll do it when...' mindset to kill your dream, the solution is to invest a little time to look deep within yourself to access your internal wisdom. This will help you see beyond the obvious and connect to a sense of purpose, in the form of a powerful uplifting vision that will attract whatever it is you need to get started.

On the morning I nearly died, I can't tell you exactly how much time I invested in looking within to connect to the purpose of needing to survive for my family, but it couldn't have been more than a few minutes. Whatever it was, that tiny investment of time attracted the supernatural strength I needed to fight for my life and win. At the time of writing this book, so far the return on that tiny investment of a few minutes is well over three years – three years and counting that would have been stolen from me if I had followed the train of thought and activity, or lack thereof, that this mindset was prepared to lead me down. The destination, had I done that, would almost certainly have been my premature death.

What about you? What is at risk of dying a premature death in your life? How much has this mindset stolen from you? My sincere hope is that you are not in any kind of life-or-death situation, but whatever the case may be, if you are regularly giving in to this mindset, you are in one way or another enabling it to steal, kill and destroy some of the incredible life that you are purposed to live. I want more than anything for that to end for you right now. I am passionate about seeing you rise up in order to overcome this thieving mindset and fulfil your purpose, because I believe that the more of us mums who can do that, the more we will collectively come up with solutions that will make this world a better place for all of us.

So many mums come to me close to – or already at – the point of burnout, barely having time for their family and themselves due to an overwhelming work schedule in a job they hate. Typically, when I ask why they haven't made a change I hear answers that clearly point to the 'I'll do it when...' mindset. One answer in particular that I hear regularly is, 'I will try to move into a more fulfilling role when I have more experience in that new field, so that I don't have to take a pay cut.' I have lost track of how many times I have successfully helped such women to work with the experience that they do have in their area of interest to create a more harmonious work and life situation for themselves. Often this results in more compensation in the very same company; a place in which they couldn't previously see any possibilities when they were focused on what they were lacking.

When they see how far they have come, their empathy for others often moves them to create initiatives that improve the situation of others who are struggling like they were. Some of my clients have won awards and been featured in international media for the incredible work they have gone on to do to lift others up. What has made them most proud in many cases has been seeing the effect of their success on their children and family. Several of my clients have moved me to tears when they said they could finally see themselves as the role model and inspiration they had always wanted to be to their kids, all because they decided to say yes to their own desires and began to work with what little they had to move towards them.

What about you? Who will your vision lift up as you rise? Give yourself the satisfying gift of discovering this as you create and step into your uplifting vision as we continue our journey together.

## Exact steps to take to overcome this dream killer

Whether you can see this mindset operating in your life or not, here are some simple steps you can take right now to overcome it and ensure it is not robbing you of time or anything else. First, you want to create an uplifting vision based on your powerful internal wisdom. What are those things you really want to do for yourself that you keep putting off? Maybe you want to get into more fulfilling work, get in better shape, or even write a book. Whatever it is, resist the urge to wait until some more perfect moment. Instead, I invite you to use this process to create an uplifting vision that motivates you into action now. Once you have your vision of the thing it is you are seeking, the next steps are to complete a Getting Started exercise, and to instil simple, ongoing weekly and daily habits. These steps will keep you on track and ensure you're not just spending or, worse, wasting time, but also deliberately investing some of your time in a way that gets you a massive return in terms of fulfilment and success.

## Creating your uplifting vision

So, what do we actually need to do to create this vision, and what does it take to make it uplifting? How can we tap into this powerful internal wisdom? These are questions I hear often from women, which I will be answering here, starting with how to tap into your internal wisdom.

This is a pretty simple thing to do, but it's not always easy to fit it into these busy lives we lead. However, as the return on investing time doing this can be so massive, it's incredibly worthwhile to find the time to be intentional about it. Tapping into your internal wisdom works in exactly the same way as going about tapping into wisdom from others – you truly listen, and if you're anything like me, take notes where possible. In this age of endless demands from our kids, work, partners – everyone – it can be so easy to fall into the trap of listening to everybody else but ourselves. That small voice within us that we just know is telling us what is best for ourselves often gets ignored as we give in to the screaming demands coming from all around us.

As we have seen, it can be extremely costly to keep ignoring *you*, so take time to listen. I have found journaling to be a fantastic way to do this. It doesn't need to be complicated; I simply mean grabbing a pen and notebook and retreating somewhere quiet enough to hear that still small voice within you. I start by setting the intention to connect to the most aligned and powerful wisdom for my situation, then I ask great questions of myself and just write whatever comes up. As I freely journal whatever springs to mind, I usually feel a sense of empowerment and inspiration when I have written something that is powerful wisdom or instruction for right now. I don't know how else to describe it when this happens, other than that I just know that what I wrote is profound and not to be ignored, even if it is as simple as the instruction I received from within on the morning I nearly died: 'Look up to the left'.

If you don't already practise journaling, I encourage you to begin. An amazing place to start, or to continue, using this practice is to create your uplifting vision. Simply grab your journal and a pen, then set the intention to connect with the deepest, most aligned desires of your soul by journaling on these questions:

**If absolutely anything was possible, and there were no limitations, what kind of life would I create?**

And, secondly, but just as importantly, *Why?*

Imagine yourself with a blank canvas on which you can create a work of art – one that is your very best life, in which you, your family and all your responsibilities are exceptionally well taken care of. I'd love for you to dream big and go wild with this – take off your 'realistic' hat for this exercise if you need to. By that I mean stop listening to that other voice we can sometimes hear within us; the voice that tells us we're not good enough, or that we don't have enough of whatever it is that we need. It often tells us that what we really want is not realistic or even possible, so it's best to tone things down to what is realistic.

If my life and experiences have taught me anything, it's that sometimes 'realism' is overrated. Anything is possible for those who are ready to believe that and go for it. I have seen impossible dreams come true for me, have helped others achieve them, and I will show you, step by step, how to do the same in your life as you continue through this book.

So, go ahead, write out your wildest 'if anything was possible' vision and why it means so much to you to be able to live this life. Your 'why' is what makes the vision uplifting enough to get you started. It will also motivate you when the going gets tough, and keep you focused on the right activities.

There are a couple more things I would love for you to incorporate as you thoughtfully complete this exercise: first, consider how you can create a vision that puts you in a better position than you would have been in had you not struggled with some of your challenges in the first place. Few things are more satisfying than 'payback' for your troubles – trust me. For example, I have used my story about what was a terrifying near-death experience to benefit my work greatly, by using it to inspire and encourage women all over the world that there is no challenge that is insurmountable, so they too can start to create and live their best lives. Few things give me more satisfaction.

In the same way, I encourage you to find ways to make your current troubles pay you back as you create your vision. To help with this, as you journal ask yourself questions like *what good can come out of this?*, or thoughtfully complete the sentence, *I'm glad this happened because...* These reflections will help you get some 'payback' ideas flowing.

Finally, as you create your 'if anything was possible' vision and the 'why' behind it, I advise you to begin to build a holistic picture. Rather than just focusing on one aspect of your life, create the vision that has you living your version of your very best life, in which you are taking amazing care of yourself, your family and all that relates to your personal and professional goals. What's your dream life vision for you personally, for your work, family and everything else? Design a masterpiece to work towards in each area of your life. Get intricate with the details of all the things that matter to you for yourself, not just for everyone else. For example, my vision currently includes regularly getting at least seven hours of sleep a night so that I can feel rested enough to get my workout in and avoid feeling tired, which I know makes me more likely to be cranky and irritable around my kids. What does it look like for you? Connect with the deepest desires of your soul and write from that place without any thoughts of limits.

A couple of other techniques you might find helpful for this, in addition to journaling, are visualising and meditating, which will help you get to your most uplifting and exciting vision. To practise these, close your eyes and do whatever you can to shut out all the noise from your physical senses. Then, from that space, begin to imagine and walk through what it would be like to already be living in your vision – what would it look like, smell like, feel like, and so on. As you do this, you are more open to receive flashes of inspiration and new ideas from the wisdom within you to implement and accelerate your progress in the time you have.

Such priceless guidance is rarely available to women who are constantly in reaction mode to life – who don't know what they want – or to those who are waiting for when they have time to get started.

To illustrate what this visualisation and meditation could look like, imagine for a minute that you had to get a present for a special friend's birthday. If you have no idea what to buy and are so busy that you spend no time thinking about what might be a wonderful gift for her, the chances are that what you do end up getting, if anything, will not be that great. If, however, you took time to envision and visualise how you want her to feel and react, and meditate on what would get that reaction, you might receive an inspired memory from within you, like, *She loves lilies!* That would give you the idea to go online to see about having lilies delivered to her. As you log on to order the delivery, you see a special offer notification on the website – for every order of lilies you can also have a luxury box of chocolates delivered for free! You're so thrilled because you know she loves those chocolates too. So, you quickly buy the gift that is guaranteed to get the incredible reaction you envisioned. See what I mean?

It's the same with our lives: as we get clear on what we want and take time to focus on creating it with practices like journaling, visualisation and meditation, we open ourselves up to divine downloads of insight that lead to incredible manifestations of the vision in real life; often better than those we had envisioned.

So, go ahead and create your most incredible vision using these techniques. When you have it, continue on to the Getting Started exercise outlined below, along with the daily and weekly habits. These activities will help you to create and begin to step into your vision, starting with whatever small moments of time or other resources that you have to work with. No matter what it looks like, you always have enough to get started.

## Getting Started exercise

Once you have your big, uplifting vision created, if you're anything like many of the clients I have worked with, it may feel overwhelming, and perhaps totally impossible, because of how different it is from the life you are living now. Like many of them, you may be wondering, *how will I ever find time for this?* or, *it already felt like twenty-four hours a day was not enough to survive in my life, how I am supposed to find time to work on this vision of thriving you've led me to create, Maxine?* The honest truth is that you probably won't be able to find the time for it if you continue living the way you have been. That's why you need to instil new daily and weekly success habits that will lead you to where you want to go. As is the case with any journey, it helps to know where you are starting from, so that you can plan the most effective route. That is what this exercise is all about. It will help you assess where you are and what the best next steps are to begin to move towards your uplifting vision. I recommend you complete it over the next week, then begin the process of instilling the weekly and daily habits below. This simple but powerful exercise will help you to see how twenty-four hours a day can finally be enough, by introducing you to a couple of the powerful concepts I teach the amazing women in my coaching programmes.

The first concept will expose where and how you are being robbed of time. Identifying the things that cause you to feel like a hamster on a wheel with your never-ending to-do list. The second will show you how to go from just 'spending' or being 'robbed' of time to becoming a 'deliberate investor' of your time in a way that reaps the return of realising your uplifting vision.

## Step 1: Exposing where you are being robbed of time

This can be such a gamechanger. Often when we feel like twenty-four hours is not enough, that's not actually the case; it's usually the work of the dream killers – those deep-rooted issues that cause us to focus on the thoughts and activities that rob us of our time, usually without us realising that they are the real culprits. To be able to deal with them effectively, we must bring the devastating effects of their theft to light.

This exercise involves taking an honest, non-judgemental look at how you are currently using your twenty-four hours each day, so that the changes you need to make are crystal clear in order to enable you to achieve the pace and productivity of the life you envision. You can do this by tracking how you are using your time in the way that is simplest for you. It doesn't have to be a work of art – it could be a straightforward list that looks something like:

**6:30am**: Wake up.
**6:30–6:45am**: Quick check of emails, news and social media.
**6:45–7:00am**: Coffee and getting the kids' breakfasts and lunches ready.
**7:00–7:30am**: Shower and get dressed.

Keep going and map out the rest of the day – whatever it looks like for you from the moment you wake up right until you fall asleep at night. Track your time in this way for one full week. It doesn't have to be perfect, and no one but you has to see it; you just need to be able to look back and understand what you've written in each daily time log by the end of the week. Some people prefer to use a piece of paper to write things down, others prefer to use apps, or simply take notes on their phone. There is no right or wrong way, pick whatever is quickest and easiest for you; the last thing we want is for this exercise to get so cumbersome that you give up on it.

Please don't skip this step, even if you have done this or something similar before. I highly recommend that you give yourself the gift of doing this over the next week. It could potentially blow your mind by exposing the huge ways in which dream killers are robbing you of time and so much else. This will then allow you to get some quick wins before you even get started with your new weekly and daily habits.

What we are trying to achieve with this exercise is to expose the impact that dream killers are having on your life (the symptoms), so that as you tackle the root cause (the dream killers themselves), you know exactly where you can expect time to be freed up throughout your week in order to focus on you and your goals. The symptoms of dream killers typically manifest as activities that you perform unconsciously, which basically rob you of time that you would not choose to consciously spend on them. In my experience of doing this exercise, and working with clients on this, I have found that most of our actions happen on autopilot without us giving them much conscious thought.

After doing this exercise for just two days, one of my precious clients, a beautiful mum who had been struggling for years to find time for exercise and self-care to lose weight and improve her health, discovered that she was spending an average of five hours a day in total on Netflix and social media. She was shocked – especially by the nearly three hours she was spending on social media on average each day. Her conscious mind had assumed that she was popping into Facebook and Instagram for a couple of minutes to check on a few notifications, a handful of times a day. In actual fact, it was typically well over a dozen times a day for more than ten minutes each time. She felt terrible, not just at the sheer amount of time being robbed from her, but because of how the activity impacted her. Her time on social media often involved her comparing herself to other mums, then feeling bad for 'not measuring up'.

I encouraged her to quit the comparison and the negative feelings. Now that she was armed with this information, she could make positive changes in her life, which is exactly what she did. She worked on tackling the dream killers that were driving this behaviour with the same tools, tips and techniques I will be sharing with you in this chapter and throughout this book. As a result, she halved her Netflix time to one hour a day, then used the time saved to invest in self-care through exercise and other related activities. She went on to lose close to ten pounds in the following month, after having struggled for years to drop weight following the birth of her youngest child. She also started working on limiting her social media use to thirty minutes a day maximum, so that she could use the time saved to pursue other goals from her vision that she valued way more than keeping informed about social media highlights from everyone else's lives on Facebook.

The impact of this exercise has been so powerful for her, and I am confident it will be for you too when you have completed a week of tracking how you are using your time. There could be many ways that you are currently using your time that would surprise your conscious mind when it is laid out in black and white in the form of a week's worth of honest time logs.

Once you have this information, you are ready to go from simply being robbed of time and mindlessly spending it to becoming a deliberate investor of time that reaps the reward of making your uplifting vision a reality.

## Step 2: Go from simply spending to deliberately investing time

Before we explore more about how you can become a deliberate investor of time, I think it's probably worth me explaining a bit more about what I mean by that. Let's shift our focus momentarily from time to money to help me make the point. Think about spending versus investing money. At a very simplified level, we spend money on all the things we want and need. If we want some sort of return on our money, however, in order to create a better lifestyle in the future, we typically don't achieve that by just spending all our money now; we usually look for a way to invest some of it in the hopes that, in the future, our delayed gratification will enable us to reap the returns we want.

In the same way, if we want to create and step into our vision, we can't just 'go with the flow', wasting and spending all our time mindlessly – we need to deliberately invest some of it in ways that will help us reap the return of our realised vision. Sadly, so many mums who hope to someday stop being so overwhelmed, and who are wishing and hoping for a better future, will never get there unless drastic changes are made. If you look at how they spend their time, they don't have the slightest hope of ever creating anything better, until they are perhaps forced to by something awful like burnout. Please don't let that be you.

Once you have a full week of time tracking, I'd love to invite you to take a few minutes to give yourself an honest review of each activity you logged. Next to each line I want you to write down 'wasted', 'spent' or 'invested'. Write down 'wasted' if it was an activity that somehow took you further away from your vision. Write 'spent' if it was an activity in which your time was just spent, meaning it didn't really take you closer to or further away from your vision. Finally, write down 'invested' if it was an activity in which you invested your time – that is, if it was an action that somehow helped you to move closer to your vision.

I want to make a couple of comments to help you avoid some common pitfalls that can be encountered when doing this exercise. First, please note that this activity is not meant to make you feel bad or condemned for 'spending' or 'wasting' a lot of your time. I am not here to sell you on some sort of right or wrong proportion of time spent or invested. It's different for everyone because we are all unique, with our own individual journeys and purpose. The main point of this exercise is to bring awareness of your starting point; to notice where your time is currently going so that you can consciously decide what changes may be needed to get you from this starting point to where you want to go. Second, remember that this process is geared towards you being able to create a weekly schedule that helps you to step into an uplifting and empowering vision for your whole life, both professionally and personally.

A lot of mums make the mistake of placing more of an emphasis on time investments that help them take care of their family and to-do lists, while treating investments in themselves as unimportant. If this is you, please hear me clearly: you are extremely important. Investing in you and your self-care is also an investment in the other people and things that rely on you and your wellbeing. It's the equivalent of putting on your oxygen mask first in an emergency in a plane, and therefore one of the most caring things you can do for your loved ones. So, make sure you classify what is important for your wellbeing appropriately.

Once you are done, take a look at the lines that show time 'wasted' and 'spent'. Consider how much time you have used on those items and ask yourself whether you are happy to continue using this amount of time for these activities. If the answer is yes, great! You can continue knowing you have made the conscious decision to use your time in that way. If not, however, I invite you to work on tackling the dream killers causing them, with the strategies shared so far, below and in upcoming chapters, so you can eliminate, or at the very least reduce, time wasted and mindlessly spent on these activities, and make better time investments that bring you closer to your vision instead.

This simple one-week exercise has been so powerful for many mums I have worked with, and I believe it will be for you too. Once you have completed this, you are ready to start the powerful weekly practice of creating a success schedule.

## Weekly habits: your success schedule

Creating a weekly success schedule is a powerful investment of your time, as it can be completed relatively quickly each week, but the benefits can be life- and destiny-altering. They include helping you feel less overwhelmed, and helping you find time to do what you want and need to do for you and others. No more putting things off due to the 'I'll do it when...' mindset.

I personally like to do this activity at the end of my workday on a Friday, just before the weekend, to help me prepare for the following week. There is no right or wrong moment, the best is the one you can commit to, no matter what. I encourage you to decide now when that will be for you to do this consistently, then block out a dedicated slot every week in your calendar. It might be after you've put the kids to bed on a Sunday, or perhaps after you have had your weekly work priorities meeting. Think through what a typical week currently looks like for you and select a time that works, then commit to show up for yourself like you would an important colleague, client or family member. I recommend blocking out at least thirty minutes initially; as this becomes a habit, you can see if more or less time is needed and adjust accordingly.

Here's how I use the thirty minutes or so that I set aside for this every week. I start by looking at my vision and the various goals within it, then, for each one, I ask myself, 'If I were to achieve this, what would life look like a year from now?', then I make a note of what comes to mind. I continue, 'If that's what life looks like a year from now, what does it need to look like three months from now for me to be on track to achieve that one-year vision?' I write that down. Then I ask, 'What about in one month's time? What do I need to have achieved by then to be on track to my three-month goal?' I make a note of that too. Finally, I ask, 'If I am to hit that one-month goal, what do I need to achieve this week?' Once I have the answers to this last question, those are my purpose-driven to-dos that I need to prioritise for the week ahead.

Let me illustrate what this could look like for a specific goal. In 2020, I decided that I was finally going to make self-care a priority and lose my excess baby weight after a few previous unsuccessful attempts. In my uplifting vision, I was going to be in the best shape of my life physically within the next year. This meant that, over the next three months, the goal was to lose approximately ten kilograms, or twenty-two pounds. If I was to be successful with that, my one-month vision was to lose approximately three kilograms, or a little over seven pounds. To be on track to hit that in a month, each week I needed to lose a little under a kilogram, or 1 3/4 pounds. With that, I then worked out my purpose-driven to-dos that would enable me to be on track to reach that goal and ensured they went into my weekly schedule. For this weight-loss example, those purpose-driven to-dos were to get and follow the guidance of my online sports nutritionist along with a fitness coach who knew that I only had fifteen to twenty minutes a day to exercise.

Can you see how simple it is? You want to do the equivalent of that for the goals in your vision with whatever time and resources you have to work with, while also avoiding falling prey to the 'I'll do it when...' mindset. For the exercise example above, my fitness coaching programme ideally required thirty to thirty-five minutes each day, but all I could find in my schedule was fifteen to twenty minutes, so I did that, and it still worked well.

Another quick side note: I don't recommend trying to work on too many goals at the same time, as that will inevitably lead to overwhelm and defeat the purpose. It's pretty important to discover what the priority areas to focus on should be for you right now at this point in your life, then stick to those no matter what others around you are thinking or doing. I have personally found that I usually only have the capacity to focus on a small handful of major goals at a time – at most three. If I look around at friends and family and start feeling like I need to do the same things they are doing or, even worse, actually *try* to start doing the same things I see them doing when my purpose does not call me to focus on that right now, guilt and overwhelm can begin to creep in and rob me of more time and quality of life. I encourage you to focus on your goals in the same way. You can access your internal wisdom through journaling to decide which goals within your vision you should focus on at any given time.

Once you are clear on the aspects of your vision that you feel led to focus on currently, break down each goal within those into your purpose-driven to-dos for the week, just as I did in the weight-loss example above.

Once you have all your purpose-driven to-dos, you will no doubt have other things that you have to do. Create a full list of all your to-do items, including things like eating, sleeping, whatever you need to do for your kids, other family members, and so on. Literally list everything you are aware that you will have to do in the week ahead. This should be easy to pull from the one-week activity tracker above that I had you complete to help you see how you are currently using your time. You are now ready to run the full to-do list through what I like to think of as my 5D weekly success schedule process.

## The 5D weekly success schedule process

The five Ds in this process are *Delete*, *Delegate*, *Don't*, *Do* and *Decide*. Here's what they mean and how to implement this process each week.

### Delete

First, as you look at your full list of to-dos, I encourage you to *Delete* anything that is not leading you towards your vision, or that you are not willing to consciously spend time on. Of course, your purpose-driven to-dos shouldn't be removed, as they are leading you to your vision, so focus more on the other things that you have on your to-do list. It's also worth restating my point that you are welcome to leave things on the list that are not necessarily leading you to your vision if you are happy to spend time on them. For example, some of my clients have left things like a particular TV series they want to keep up with on their list, as a self-care treat at the end of the day, or going out to dinner, or even shopping with friends, because they value the relationships and want to nurture them. If there is something like that that you really value or enjoy, and you feel that to completely eliminate it would be detrimental to your overall wellbeing, by all means leave it on. In a way, it is leading to your vision, which no doubt includes your wellbeing, so feel free to make such conscious choices for yourself and delete the others. For example, you might want to delete staying late at the office, even when you are finished with the work that has to be done there, because that's the unspoken expectation in your team. Another example of something I personally deleted that freed up hours for me each day was the need to stay up-to-date with the messages in every single one of the dozens of WhatsApp messaging groups I am in. It was tough initially, because I care about people in the groups I had to mute, and I had serious FOMO; but when I compared what it would feel like to achieve my goals to keeping up to date, and constantly engaging with the at-times endless streams of messages, my vision won, by far.

It might feel harsh to delete things like these from your list that you used to do, especially if it involves other people that you don't want to hurt by saying no when you've perhaps said yes for years. However, you owe it to yourself to say yes to your purpose and your most aligned life journey, even if it means saying no to others at the risk of upsetting them. Chances are, they won't be as upset as you fear they will be when you tell them. But even if they are, you can use some of the strategies I will share with you on page 184 to unapologetically communicate and enforce your boundaries.

Fear of what others will do or say should never keep you from creating and living the life you were born to. The truth is, you will never manage to please everyone anyway, so why waste your time and life trying? Even if by some miracle you are the only person on the entire planet that successfully manages to please everyone, I am almost certain that on your death bed the regret of not living the life you were meant for would overshadow any satisfaction you achieved from people-pleasing.

I don't mean to be so bleak about this, but I believe so much in you and the purpose you are here for, so I want to stress the importance of this. You literally can't afford to keep ignoring your internal wisdom in an attempt to please others. The same people you are sacrificing your own needs for are very likely the ones that would be most adversely impacted by you not living out your full purpose, as this can, and often does, lead to feelings of resentment towards them as you become increasingly unfulfilled. Research shows that the best way to empower our kids to live a purpose-driven and fulfilled life is to model it for them – if they see us constantly sacrificing ourselves for the benefit of others, the chances are they will believe in the necessity to replicate that in their own lives. So please, find the courage to delete the activities that don't lead you towards achieving your vision, no matter the cost. Once you are done with the deleting, you may discover that your to-do list is already starting to look so much more manageable, and you are now finding time for a lot of those things you were putting off until you had more time.

## Delegate

You are now ready for the next D, which is **Delegate**. Just because something needs to be done, it doesn't mean it has to be done by you. Please re-read that last line – read it repeatedly if you have to, until it really sinks in. This is such a huge source of stress for so many mums I've worked with, starting with me. We feel that if we don't do it, no one will, or that if someone else does it, they won't do it anywhere near as well as we would. So we either procrastinate on more important things until the elusive moment 'when we have time', or continue on, frustrated at our hamster wheel of a life, trying, and failing, to do the impossible task of completing our never-ending to-do list. We then often start feeling resentful towards the very people that we are doing it all for.

This cycle is not sustainable and makes no sense. So please, let others help. If you are in the position where you don't have many people, or even anyone, to ask for help from, my heart goes out to you. I can relate to this, as can some of my clients and friends.

The key if you are in this situation is to avoid giving in to the 'I'll do to it when...' mindset, which will keep you doing everything and never getting round to delegating. To overcome this, switch your focus from what you are lacking – in this case, obvious support sources, to what it is that you do have, then begin to work with that, no matter how small it may seem. Some of the incredible single mums I have worked with over the years who did not have a partner or close family to delegate to *did* have friendships in place – people who have become more like family when the woman reached out to ask for help. For one mum of two, where even that was not possible, rather than focus on who she didn't have available, she focused on who she *did* have: her two children – a seven-year-old and a three-year-old with special needs who required a lot from her, in addition to everything else she had to do. As there was literally no one else to delegate to, she began to enlist her seven-year-old to help with some of the basic tasks at home. She was initially nervous about whether this would be placing too much responsibility on them too early, but instead she found that it was one of the best things she could ever have done for her family. Not only was the burden of these small tasks lifted from her, but her older child, who had been feeling overlooked due to all the attention their younger sibling was receiving, was now feeling more empowered, significant and important – they absolutely love helping her out, and they are thriving at school and at all their other activities that their mum was scared would suffer. Like so many of us, the mum was worried that by delegating, things wouldn't be done exactly as she would have done them. However, she also found out that even if someone else doesn't do something exactly as we would have done it, some level of completion is far better than it being left on our stress-inducing list of things we are kidding ourselves that we will get round to doing at some point. If you can relate to that concern, you might even be surprised to find that some tasks may get done better than you would have done them if you give others a chance and hand them over.

When I first started my business I literally did everything, and so, unsurprisingly, things became overwhelming pretty quickly. I finally decided that I needed to hire someone to support me in the running of the business, someone to whom I could assign some of the tasks. Even though I could theoretically do them all myself, it simply wasn't possible for me to continue doing everything necessary to keep my business afloat along with all the other commitments that I was juggling in my life. I was worried that the person I hired would not be able to do these jobs as well as I could, but I resolved to give her a try for the sake of my wellbeing and sanity. She ended up being brilliant, alleviating so much stress and overwhelm, and allowing me to be so much more successful in all areas of my life. She not only did some of the tasks far better than I could have, but she also went above and beyond to show incredible initiative, which even led to my work and business being featured in international media. This then paved the way for other incredible media features that have not only benefitted me, but also many thousands of readers and viewers around the world. This amazing expansion of my vision would never have happened if I hadn't allowed myself to be both vulnerable and strong enough to finally ask for help. I invite you to do the same – who knows what surprising paths could open up for you as a result? I'm excited for you to find out!

To implement this Delegate step, simply look through the

remaining to-dos on your list and ask yourself questions like, 'Who else can do this?', or, 'How can I get help with this?', then access your internal wisdom as needed. Once you get some ideas, I encourage you to delegate some of these tasks by giving clear expectations of the outcome you want, then releasing control of how the tasks get done. Allow people to leverage their own strengths and ways of doing things.

If it is feasible, you could enlist paid help, or ask for help from others, like friends, family, neighbours and colleagues, if it makes sense to do so and they are available. You would be amazed at how many people are willing to help. Please don't try to be 'superwoman', she is likely exhausted and only showing you 1 per cent of her life through her social media highlights. Asking for help of any sort is not a sign of weakness but of strength, and wisdom.

## Don't

Now that you have hopefully got rid of much of your to-do list in the last two steps, I invite you to consider the third D – **Don't** – by which I mean, don't use a to-do list as a plan for what you will be doing each day. If you're a to-do-list lover, like I was and many of my clients are, please don't panic; hear me out. There are a couple of reasons why I advise against using to-do lists as the main way of managing our time and activities. The first is the false sense of productivity they may give. Whether it's the to-do list in our heads, on our phones or on paper, many of us love the satisfaction of making these lists and crossing things off because we have been conditioned to believe that as we cross things off, we can feel good because we are being productive. But what if keeping a running to-do list actually makes us less productive? Have you ever had a day where you are busy crossing things off your list, and then at the end of it you still feel like you have so much to do? When we keep such never-ending to-do lists, they can make us feel stressed and as though we are never doing enough, resulting in us feeling frustrated, beating ourselves up, and concluding that we have no time to fit in new activities that can lead us to our vision. All of this inevitably ends up negatively impacting our mental health and productivity.

The other reason why I don't recommend using these lists, at least not exclusively, is that when we live our lives in this way we tend to take on and say yes to more than is humanly possible to ever get done. It's no wonder that twenty-four hours a day does not feel like enough, because it simply isn't – at least, not to get done all that we have committed to do. What I recommend instead is that you schedule your remaining to-dos (after deleting and delegating) in order of priority to you, right into a calendar or scheduling system at the actual times that you will complete each activity. That way, it's crystal clear exactly what is humanly possible for you to complete in the seven twenty-four-hour days ahead. This will make it less likely that you overcommit and instead will assist you in being realistic about when and how you will be able to get stuff done. This approach also helps you avoid putting yourself under undue pressure by accepting deadlines that are too tight, based on what you already have scheduled.

I don't recommend any particular calendar system, just whatever works best for you. Some of my clients like to write in a physical planner with a calendar, others like apps or online calendars. Find what works for you; the key thing is being able to deliberately plan how you will be investing and spending your time in the week ahead, so that in addition to looking after everything and everyone you are responsible for, you are also moving towards your personal vision with each day. As you do this, you're also not kidding yourself about what you can actually get done by working through a stress-inducing to-do list that is never actually completed.

Living with this sort of vision and purpose-driven schedule each week is powerful for so many reasons. One of my favourites is how I use it to co-create a true partnership with my husband. As a dual-career couple with kids, things can get challenging at times, with all the childcare and unpaid housework. I personally like to use an online calendar for my weekly success schedule, and when I plan ahead each week, I send my husband calendar invites for the times when I have key meetings and activities. This makes him aware of when I am busy, and the activities I need his support for, which we then discuss and finalise logistics for. He also lets me know when he is busy with important activities in the same way, so that I can support him. Thus we avoid potential conflicts that don't work with my own schedule. It takes communication and ongoing tweaking to keep this working, but it helps us avoid the default suggestion from society that it should be me as the mother who automatically takes on most of the unpaid work at home.

Living by your calendar is also really great if you are a people-pleaser who struggles to say no to others, like I was. When people ask you to do things, if you have your weekly success schedule in place you can honestly respond by saying, 'Sorry, I'm totally booked,' or offer a time in the coming weeks that makes sense if you do want to help. This way, you are helping them but not sacrificing your own vision and purpose in the process. Finally, it is also really helpful to live like this if you are someone who struggles with distractions. One of my clients, who was trying to limit the amount of time she spent on social media each day, found it so much easier to be disciplined with her fifteen minutes a day limit when she had her success schedule in place. When tempted to mindlessly browse through her various social media feeds like she normally did, she would instead glance at her success schedule, check what she was actually supposed to be doing, and think about the result she was working towards with that activity. She would then ask herself, is the trade-off worth it? Do I really want to give up on or slow down my progress towards this goal for social media time? The answer was usually no.

## Do

Once you have the week ahead planned as best you know how to in your weekly success schedule, you are ready to get started on the fourth D, which is *Do*. Do the activities at the scheduled time, leveraging your strengths to increase your effectiveness and efficiency. If, for example, you have excellent people and communication skills, be deliberate about using these strengths to make tasks like work meetings more interesting and efficient. Similarly, you want to be intentional about leveraging your strengths outside of work. If you are great at planning and organising, use this strength to your advantage; for instance, rather than making one meal in the slot you have assigned for cooking on one day, you could cook a larger amount and store extra portions for a few more meals at a later time, thus saving you prep and effort on another busy night. Alternatively, as you put away your laundry, you could plan out outfits for the week to save time wondering what to wear each day.

## Decide

Finally, as you go through the week, use the final D, which is *Decide*, as necessary. You need to decide what to do with any new activities and requests for your time that come up. As lovely as it would be to create your weekly success schedule and have everything go according to plan, that almost never happens. Things come up – someone could get sick, you get a call from a friend who needs a favour, your boss may want you to do some additional overtime, you get invited to an event, or some other random change of plan occurs. Whatever it is, try to run through the 5D process to decide if and how it gets done.

Let's illustrate this with the example of your boss giving you some additional work mid-week. For the first D (Delete), you will want to check whether this new activity is leading you towards your vision, and if not, whether you are willing to consciously spend time on it. In this case, assuming that the request is a fair one, based on your role and responsibilities, and doing a great job is in line with your vision, this is obviously not a task that you can delete. If the request is something that requires your personal skills and input, it's not one that you would delegate, either. Instead, given that your calendar is already full for the week, you can check back with your boss to see whether it's acceptable to deliver this new project next week, or whether she would prefer you to move some of your tasks from tomorrow out to next week to free up time for this new task. Once she confirms her priorities about which tasks need to be done first, you can make the necessary tweaks in your calendar and keep working through the schedule. It's that simple – and stress-relieving.

## Your daily success habits

I now want to share some helpful daily habits that, if practised consistently, will increase your results exponentially. With any change you are trying to make, the key is consistency. You need to do something so regularly that it becomes normal and automatic, in the same way as brushing your teeth. For most people, this is not something we have to think about: it just gets done, usually on autopilot, twice a day. That's what we're aiming for with this strategy: intuitively and automatically leaning into the powerful wisdom within you, and taking intentional actions towards the uplifting vision it leads you to, no matter how busy life gets due to other demands.

It's a common belief that it takes twenty-one days to form a new habit, but based on my experience working with mums over several years, I have found that it actually takes a bit longer for things to stick and become automatic. I would say that two to three months is the average length of time I have seen it take to build the necessary consistency with these practices and for women to see radical results in their lives. It may be more or less for you personally, depending on how far from the average you fall. I want to make clear that if you resolve to stick with this no matter how long it takes, you will see incredible results in your life.

Often when we get started with something like a weekly schedule, things pop up that make it difficult to stick to. If you have really young kids, it's highly unlikely they'll think, *Oh, Mum has started using a weekly schedule, I'd better allow her the time to implement it.* All the overwhelming demands that were there before you started trying to implement this will still be there, challenging your ability to continue to reach the point where it becomes normal and automatic. So, what exactly do you need to do to keep going with this? I suggest you include a non-negotiable slot of around thirty minutes every day in your schedule over the next three months at least to build these habits of leaning into your intuition and inner wisdom and taking action towards your vision. If you can't find thirty minutes, start with whatever time is realistic. Small things, when used intentionally, can lead to mighty things.

Before I share more details of what you'll be doing in this time, the first thing I would say is make sure that this time is scheduled in your calendar as one of the most important items of the day – if not *the* most. As before, choose a time that makes the most sense for you and that you will consistently show up for. I personally do it first thing in the morning, right after I get up. I set my alarm to wake up a bit earlier than my husband and kids so that I won't be disturbed. I love this time, as the house is peaceful and quiet and my mind is yet to be influenced by any of the news and activity from the day. In this moment I can more easily tune in to my inner wisdom and guidance without distractions, and I usually feel extremely empowered afterwards, which I find is an incredible way to go through the rest of my day. It's an extremely effective morning routine for me.

Whether you decide to do this in the morning or at another time of the day, there are three simple steps I'd suggest you complete in order to come away from this time feeling inspired, empowered and motivated to have a productive day. The first thing is to remind yourself that the uplifting vision you are working towards is possible for you. The goal as you complete this first step is to transcend the limitations and frustrations that may currently exist in your life, and to connect back to a powerful sense of purpose and strength in order to overcome it all. You can do this in just a few minutes, by deliberately deciding what you choose to believe. There is a famous quote attributed to Henry Ford that I love: 'Whether you think you can, or you think you can't, you're right.' My clients and I use this to our benefit every day, and you can too. The mind and what you choose to believe can help you overcome whatever obstacles you are facing in your life. This also works in the opposite way – if you believe something negative, you are far more likely to see that thing occurring in your day-to-day life.

So, how do you actually apply all this to your life on a daily basis? You revisit your vision and your personal why, and you choose to believe that it is possible for you, no matter what is happening in your life and the world. Do whatever it takes to reinforce that belief; the techniques of journaling, visualisation and meditation I shared with you earlier are extremely effective for this. I enjoy using short, guided meditations, which lead me to close my eyes and visualise myself having already accomplished my goals. This practice makes me feel much closer to reaching my goals by the time I open my eyes. Some other things that help me reinforce my belief that my dreams are possible include reading stories or seeing pictures of others who have succeeded at what I am trying to achieve. I also place aspirational pictures that reinforce the beliefs that what I want is possible in places where I can see them regularly throughout the day. This step of my morning routine can usually be completed in about fifteen minutes. Find what helps you to feel empowered and in no doubt that your dreams are not only possible, but inevitable.

Once you are feeling empowered by this first step, I invite you to make a habit of tapping into your internal wisdom to reassess your schedule for the day and get clear on the 'must-do' items. Again, this does not have to take long – just a few minutes. Even when you have your weekly success schedule in place, I still recommend this step for a few reasons: firstly, because other things can, and usually do, pop up and threaten to reintroduce chaos and overwhelm, so checking in to that powerful guidance on how to re-prioritise the day, if needed, is always a good idea. Second, there may be new opportunities that you were not aware of when you created the schedule that align with your goals and your purpose, especially with things moving as fast and unpredictably as they tend to. Even if your logical mind is unaware of such opportunities, your intuition often isn't. So, it is worth checking in daily to see whether there is anything you don't currently have scheduled that might be worth doing today.

Doing this could be as simple as journaling questions like:

*Are there any changes I need to make to my schedule to keep me on purpose?*
*What are my 'must-do' items for me to remain on track to reach my vision today?*
*Who or what do I need to say no to today?*

As before, write freely until you get that sense of peace. At the end of this process, I typically find that I have on average just three to four items that are clearly 'must-dos' each day, outside of the things that are needed to look after my family and other important people in my life. Everything else I manage to get done is a bonus.

I cannot stress enough how powerful and freeing this simple step can be. It's helped me and my clients release the need to be 'always on'. We can go from constantly fretting that we are always behind, with so much to do and no time to rest, to being confident that we are on track to fulfil our purpose when we complete the handful of 'must-do' items. We have found that these few items can always be completed in the time we have. They also usually move us closer to our visions much more quickly and peacefully than when we are spread thin, trying and failing to do everything, and then wasting even more time feeling terrible about that. If you constantly feel behind and under pressure to 'always be on' in an attempt to catch up, I can't wait for you to experience this freedom as you begin to implement this step.

Once you have your priorities for the day from this process, the final daily success habit is to take a few minutes to ensure you plan to complete your 'must-do' items in the most effective and efficient way. You do this by working out which steps are necessary to help you go through your day in a way that complements your natural strengths and has you showing up as the best version of yourself. The more you do you in life, the easier it is to achieve your goals.

If you do this consistently for the next three months, you will not only overcome the dream-killing 'I'll do it when…' mindset; with each day, week and month that goes by you will be creating and stepping into your best life on autopilot – an incredible life that you are enjoying and in which you are fulfilling your purpose, while taking amazing care of everything and everyone you need to.

## Key takeaways

- When you have something you want to do and you notice yourself thinking about what you need in order to be able to do it, resolve not to give in to the 'I'll do it when...' mindset.
- Switch your focus from what you don't have to whatever it is you do have, however small, and begin to work with that intentionally.
- It helps to create an uplifting vision informed by your internal wisdom, and use whatever time and resources you have to start to work towards it; you always have enough to get started.
- Use the Getting Started exercise (see page 38) to determine your starting point by assessing how you are using your time currently and to expose where you may be wasting or mindlessly spending it.
- Install the suggested weekly and daily habits to become a deliberate investor of time who can reap the rewards of creating and living out her uplifting vision.

# Chapter 2: Needing to See It to Believe It

I began my own journey along the path of creating the impossible at around the age of eighteen, under some incredibly bizarre circumstances. I had just walked into a dark, dingy, filthy room, which smelt awful, and in doing so found myself in one of the craziest situations I had ever experienced. I stood there, speechless and heart pounding, as my senses were assaulted. I don't think I had ever felt so terrified, so ashamed, so alone. *How in the world did I end up here?* I wondered. *How could my life have come to this?*

Growing up, my mum and dad took us to Sunday school at the church every week. They had worked so hard to give us the brightest future possible, and I had wanted to be a doctor, just like my cousin; to have a beautiful house, a nice husband, kids and, most of all, to make my Nigerian parents proud. Standing in that grim room, I wondered how could I have fallen so far, and so low, from those plans?

Looking back, I can see that all the rules my parents had in place were there in order to protect me and my siblings, especially after they moved us from Nigeria to a totally new world, and culture, in London. At the time, though, it felt like control, and I wanted none of it. So, after years of bottling up my emotions as an extremely shy and introverted child, I wanted to be free, and one afternoon, after a blazing row, I ran away from home. I never thought that my fight, and flight for freedom that bright sunny day, would lead me to this dark place where I felt more trapped than ever before, or to the horrifically low point I'd reached by the time I walked into that room.

In a little over a year, I was homeless, on drugs, out of school, and so out of options that I'd agreed to the suggestion of meeting the pimp who now stood in front of me and my friend, offering us a job. Dating the wrong guy, followed by more stupid decisions, one after the other, will do that to you, I guess. Earlier in the day, it had seemed like a good idea, but the realisation of what I was really getting myself into hit me like a ton of bricks once I walked through the door into the dark, foul-smelling flat. I started to panic. I must have blacked out or something, because the next thing I remember was him snapping me out of a trance asking, 'You do know how much you're supposed to charge, right?!' Oh, dear! I had no clue. I mean, what's the going rate for this sort of thing in the late 1990s? I had no idea; my last job had been in the coffee shop at the shopping centre. So I just stood there, mouth open with no sound coming out, visibly shaking with terror, heart beating loud and fast. *I can't do this… I just can't do this…* I kept thinking, over and over.

It was like he could read my mind, because he looked at me with obvious fury and disgust and said, 'What choice do people like you have anyway?' At that, I closed my eyes tight, fighting back hot tears. I think a slap in the face would have hurt less. He was right. The painful truth was that I was a complete mess. I had ruined my life and let down everyone who cared about me. I had nothing to my name but the last three pound coins in my pocket, and no one to call. As I stood there, not sure where to look or what to do, frenzied questions flew through my mind: *How can this be my life? How could I let this happen? How in the world do I get out of this?*

As I pondered on that last question, I heard a voice within me say, 'This is not who you are meant to be, you are meant for so much more!' I had no idea who, or what, that voice was, but I wanted so desperately for what it said to be true, so I chose to believe it. That inner voice gave me the courage I needed to peel my feet off the floor, turn, and run full speed out of the flat into the freezing cold Soho street outside. Cold air had never felt so good or smelt so fresh. My excitement and relief to be out of that hellhole was short-lived, however. As I looked around me, down the dark streets, now deserted except for a few groups of people clearly up to no good, the gravity of the perilous and dire situation I was in hit me. As I worried about what to do, the fear was almost suffocating.

I walked around that night so frightened, wondering, *What next? Now what do I do?* That guy's words kept ringing in my ears: 'What choice do people like you have anyway?'

I didn't know anyone else living this crazy lifestyle who had done anything worthwhile with their lives. I was almost certain the friend I went to see him with would end up working for him, as so many others like us had done. For such girls, things never seemed to end well – some just disappeared, never to be heard from again. I wasn't even sure whether they were still alive. I didn't want to end up like them, but what could I do? I literally had no idea where to start. I had been awful to my family, so I was not ready to face them. I had dropped out of school, stopped going to church, and disconnected from any 'normal' friends. I had screwed up everything, and I really couldn't see a way out of the rock bottom of a hole that I had dug myself into. I felt so stuck, and scared. Unsure of what else to do, I went to hide in one of the red telephone boxes on the street.

Time passed slowly as I sat there, shivering, hugging my legs close to my chest to stay warm, and watching the Soho night life go by through tear-filled eyes. The terror seemed to be coming in waves that hit me with increasing intensity as I pondered my predicament. One moment during the night, it all got too much, and I suffered a panic attack fretting about what I would do when I finally ran out of money. How would I be able to pay for food and the things I had become addicted to? I closed my eyes and wondered whether I should just admit defeat and go back to that guy. *Would it be so bad if I went back there?* In that moment, I somehow reconnected to that voice inside me that I'd heard before, and once again, from somewhere within me, I heard it: 'This is not who you are meant to be, you are meant for so much more!'

With that, a sense of peace I still can't find the words to fully explain washed over me. I just knew in that instant, that really was the truth. Even though it didn't look like it, I had options, a choice; anything was possible, and I was meant for more even if I couldn't see how. I knew I just had to resolve to reach for it and everything would become clear. Right there and then, I made a firm decision that there was no going back. I would do whatever I could to discover the more I was meant for, even if it took me until my very last breath.

As soon as I made that decision, something shifted. From the outside looking in, I was still a hot mess with practically no money and no hope of ever doing anything worthwhile with her life. On the inside, however, something fundamental had changed. I don't think I had ever felt more alive, or more full of hope. I knew instinctively how to tune back in to that voice that told me I was meant for more, so I asked it, what next? How do I get this more I'm meant for? I got one word back: 'Learn'. It didn't make much sense to me, so I kept checking in and I got 'learn' over and over again.

After about an hour of this, it was starting to get light outside, with the new day dawning. I decided to leave the phone box, still talking to and trying to make sense of the voice inside me. I realised I must have looked crazy, but I didn't care. I had found what felt like a lifeline, and I was not about to let go. I don't know how long I had been walking when I stumbled into one of the most serendipitous moments I had experienced in a long time. I had heard and repeated the word 'learn' dozens of times so far that morning, so imagine my shock and delight to see the very same word in bold letters in the headlines section of a newspaper stand I was just about to walk by. I didn't even stop to register what the rest of the sentence in the headline said – I'd heard the word 'learn' enough times that morning to know without a shadow of a doubt that it was worth grabbing one of my precious pound coins from my pocket to buy the paper. I paid, got my change from the vendor, then ran to a quiet part of the street and began to read. I quickly found out that we were in what is called 'clearing' season in the UK. During this time, students were receiving their results from sixth form colleges and other institutions they attend before going to university. Typically, various universities make conditional offers about what grades you need to get from sixth form or wherever you studied before they admit you. Students who get the required grades gain admission, and those who don't get good-enough grades can use the clearing system I was learning about from the paper. Through this system you could look for and apply to universities that still have spaces on certain courses after they have admitted their first batch of students. I knew immediately that was what I was meant to do.

Tears of relief flowed down my face as I made the necessary calls, and I was eventually admitted into the University of Wales Bangor to study Banking and Finance, in spite of my terrible A level grades from the sixth form I had dropped out of. This move would not only help me get back into the school system and get my life back on track; the nearly 300-mile distance between Bangor and London meant that I would be far away from anyone who could pull me back into what I hoped would quickly become my old ways. It was a brilliant plan, and far wiser than anything I could have conjured up with my petrified logical mind that night. I was blown away at how this divine wisdom within me seemed to create a way out for me where there seemed to be none, so I kept tuning in to it and following it. Miraculously, it kept showing me the way, step by step, out of the mess I had got myself into.

I made my way to a women's shelter to get help for the basics, before returning to my family to apologise and attempt to reconcile with them. I was overwhelmed with joy and deep regret for how I had treated them as they welcomed me back with love and open arms, no questions asked. On the day I was to leave London to go to Bangor to start university, my mum and dad came along to London Euston train station to see me off. They were so proud. I cried non-stop as they helped me get my bags onto the train, hugged me, then got back onto the platform where they maintained eye contact and waved for as long as they could, even as we pulled off. I don't think I stopped crying for the nearly four-hour train journey to my new life in Bangor. They were mainly tears of deep gratitude for the unconditional love and support of my family, but also for this new approach to life that I didn't quite have the words to describe at that point. I was blown away at how I was able to access this incredible wisdom from within myself that had totally changed the trajectory of my life when I decided to follow it.

As I reflected back on this experience to write this book, I realised that this season of my life was when I encountered and overcame the dream killer of needing to see it to believe it. This dream killer effectively robs so many of us of the opportunity to create and live our best possible lives through overwhelming circumstances that suggest we have no choice but to settle for a life we really don't want. When the thought of having it all, or whatever particular thing we want, looks really hard or, worse, impossible, it's so tempting and even understandable to see no other option but to give up and settle for less, because 'what choice do people like us have?'

I was so excited to have discovered that no matter how crazy or scary things look, we don't have to just go with the flow, or settle, we always have a choice; limiting circumstances, even when self-inflicted, do not have to dictate our destiny. Tackling them with the right strategy allowed me to get to that point where I'd defied all the odds and was back on track to the more I was meant for in life, and it can do the same for you.

## Overcoming this dream killer

Do you ever feel like you are meant for more than the life you're living? Or that you have no choice but to settle and accept where you are due to your circumstances? If you answered yes to either question, chances are you're being robbed of your dreams by the dream killer of needing to see it to believe it. The sad truth is that most women I meet are victims of this approach to life, which leads us to think we have no choice but to go with the flow of our circumstances, even if we really don't want to. It's an especially effective dream killer that is often left unchallenged, because by nature there is usually very little, if any, visible evidence to suggest you will be successful in confronting it.

## How this dream killer causes us to waste time

This dream killer can take us off track and keep us away from the life we want by placing a greater weight on what we can see with our eyes compared to what we can't. We therefore spend and waste time in reaction mode, instead of in the creation mode we need to be in to be able to have it all. The vast majority of our time ends up flying by as we react to, and settle for, visible circumstances that contradict what we really want. As mums, even when we have that longing within us for more than the lives we are currently living, we focus on what we do see, and fail to access that internal wisdom that would guide us to finding a better way of life for ourselves. For so many mums, depending on our children's ages or what else we have going on, what we see keeps us busy and overwhelmed. We spend and waste so much time dealing with the visible effects of the status quo on motherhood, that we have little capacity left to challenge it. Even when things are relatively calm, and we aren't in any form of crisis, when so many of us look at the visible world around us and want more, we end up thinking something like, *Things aren't so bad, I should be grateful for what I do have.*

While I am personally all for being grateful, I am vehemently against settling for accepting a life that isn't too bad. That's because I know for a fact that it will rob you of the opportunity to have it all, as well as so much more that you couldn't possibly imagine right now. Things may not be too bad, but you have no idea how good they can get when you stop needing to see it to believe it. On that destiny-defining night in Soho in my teenage years, my only visible choice was to keep digging past rock bottom to work for that pimp. If I had gone with the flow, or entertained the thought that things were 'not too bad' – which did cross my mind – it would have very likely cost me my life in the end.

The interesting thing I have discovered since then is that no matter who you are and what you are facing, that statement is true. When you choose to settle for less than what you know you're meant for in life, you may still be breathing, but it will eventually cost you your life; that incredible, purpose-filled and fulfilling life you were born to live. When you sacrifice this best possible life, you may look fine or even great on the outside, but on the inside you'll feel like you are barely living. I sadly meet far too many women who are feeling like this and, heartbreakingly, it almost always leads to serious issues like depression, a constant comparison of themselves to others, a sense of hopelessness, and even physical illness, all because we give in to this dream killer of needing to see something outside of ourselves to validate the invisible and incredible wisdom we are getting from within us. If you are like many of the women

I have worked with, you might be wondering whether it doesn't in fact make sense to put a greater emphasis on what you can see rather than what you can't. That is a perfectly justifiable question, to which my answer is always the same: 'It depends on what it is that you want to create.'

Bearing this in mind, it may make perfect sense to focus on what you can see, but I have found that if you want to 'create the impossible' of having it all in your life and career, keeping your focus on the unseen realm is often far more powerful. For me personally, closing my eyes and choosing to focus in on one line changed the trajectory of my entire life that night in Soho: 'This is not who you are meant to be, you are meant for so much more.' Even though I had no tangible evidence of what that might mean, the thought alone helped me go from spending and wasting time reacting to horrifying circumstances on the road to nowhere to instead investing time by taking inspired action that created dramatically different circumstances. I want the same for you. No matter how terrible or fantastic your life looks on the outside right now, if internally you are settling for less than you know you are meant for, let me encourage you with that same line: 'This is not who you are meant to be, you are meant for so much more.' No matter what your circumstances look like right now, they do not need to dictate your destiny. You have always had a choice, and I am excited to help you see it, make it, and experience the incredible results that are bound to follow.

## How might this dream killer have already robbed you?

If you are like me and any of the mothers I have worked with and spoken to, this dream killer has long been at work, robbing you of the opportunity to have it all even before you became a parent. Long before we had our first child, many of us were indoctrinated with well-meaning statements like, 'Once you have kids, it's no longer about you,' or, 'Good mothers sacrifice everything for their kids.' As honourable and noble as those statements sound, to me, and to other professional women who had worked hard and invested heavily in careers they wanted to keep progressing, it was rather concerning. Perhaps you can relate. We wanted to have both a career and a family that could coexist and thrive, so because we know and have been told repeatedly about the importance of representation, we started to seek out other women who looked like us and who had both a career and a family.

What we may instead have observed for several years before ever having children was how those who were already juggling a career and a family were struggling. Niggling worries therefore took up residence in the back, and sometimes at the forefront of our minds, robbing us of the opportunity to be fully present, and maximising on the moment we were in. We worried that if we stopped to have kids, we would lose momentum in our careers and be replaced in the workforce, as we could see was happening all around us. We wanted to avoid the hefty motherhood penalty we'd seen so many women pay through reduced contributions and compensation in their career when they had children. That's before we even considered the potential loss of freedom in our personal lives that motherhood would inevitably bring. We fretted about how our future children would impact our ability to do other things we wanted to do for ourselves, such as travelling and having time for self-care. Looking at the evidence all around us, so many women, myself included initially, have concluded that having both a thriving family and the impactful fulfilling career we want must be totally incompatible. As a result, many of us delayed having the children we desperately wanted for fear of everything we would have to give up in exchange for the new title of mum.

When we finally decided to go for it, and received the incredible blessing of becoming a mother, despite all the love, joy and fulfilment that came with that, many of us sadly also received the memo that our pre-motherhood fears were totally justified. We joined millions of other mums around the world who are deeply grateful for the precious lives we have been entrusted with, while simultaneously grieving aspects of our lives we felt we had no choice but to give up. In this challenging search for balance, so many of us mums reluctantly decide to scale back or even leave our careers for the sake of our physical and mental health. Rather than feeling better mentally, however, the time spent watching our peers continue to progress in their careers leaves us feeling lost, empty and unfulfilled.

If you are anything like me and other women I've worked with, at this point you may have started to think that you have no right to complain – your life isn't too bad, and from the outside looking in, things look pretty good, maybe even really great. You've done your best to get to this point in your career, you've achieved so much, you're so lucky and blessed, but if you're honest, just between you and me, there are some moments when you feel anything but lucky on the inside. Between the running to-do list, having to be the one that always has to take care of everything and everyone, and having to constantly put yourself last and settle for less than you truly want, you're more likely to feel exhausted, overwhelmed, stressed, and at times even resentful.

Then, of course, on top of that you start to feel super guilty for feeling that way, as you ask yourself, 'What good mother feels like that? I *should* feel grateful!' It gets even worse when you see how well other mums seem to be doing compared to you. A quick scroll through your social media feed is enough to confirm one of your biggest fears; you're not good enough, nowhere near as good as you *should* be. You start to think, *I'm a bad mum. My kids deserve better. If only I didn't scream at them so much, or if only I could find time for all those amazing activities my friends, and the other perfect mums, with their perfect homes and perfect little lives, manage to find the time to do.* But there are all these other things you have to do! Work, stuff around the house, so many things in your head to get done. So, you feel like a terrible mother, if not the worst one ever. The last thing you want is to look terrible as well, so you try to find time for self-care and to make an effort. But the minute you find time to rest, or to do something just for you, you sense that nagging feeling in the back of your mind again – that it is selfish, or that there is something more important that you need to be doing. I mean, your to-do list isn't going to take care of itself, is it?

So, you sacrifice what you want for yourself over and over again because they say that's what good mums *should* do. All the while you feel anything but good and continue living this experience that is a far cry from what you hoped you'd be living by now. You spend time wondering how your life got to this and speculating on what it is that those perfect mums have or know that you don't.

If you can relate to any of this, know that you are definitely not alone, despite what social media might sometimes suggest. I for one know what it feels like to compare my everyday struggles to other people's highlight reels on social media, and it is beyond awful, not to mention that wasting time with this comparison is such an inaccurate way to measure how well we are doing. The truth is, regardless of how you feel, if you're attracted to a book like this, you are probably doing way better than you realise, or ever give yourself credit for!

The majority of women I have worked with over issues like this, including myself, tend to be so hard on themselves compared to how they perceive and treat others. We look at other people's lives with rose-tinted glasses, but we scrutinise any little imperfections in our own lives with a magnifying glass, while not giving ourselves anywhere near enough credit for the things we do really well, or the incredible wisdom within us that we can tap into. We search outside of ourselves for hope and answers and are often left feeling disappointed. In fact, one question that has come up in some way, shape or form at each of the numerous women's conferences I have spoken at over the last decade is, 'What's the secret to mums having it all in their personal lives and careers?' Most ask this hoping the answer will help them be one of the 'special few' who manage to build successful careers while raising happy families. Then they leave the conference to face the visible reality of themselves and so many other women being lost in the juggling act of working motherhood that often leaves us feeling guilty, and as if we are failing everywhere.

Wherever you are on your journey, if you have felt any of these things, let me encourage you with two thoughts: first, you are definitely not alone; millions of other mums are also in their own version of the same boat on this guilt trip with seemingly no end in sight. This may seem obvious, but I think it's definitely worth reminding you of this. One of the main things that comes up among mums from literally all over the world as they discuss their personal struggles, is, 'I thought it was just me going through this, or feeling like that.' There is something so freeing about realising others are facing similar issues and fears, and that you are not this terrible person that you have told yourself you are in your head too many times to count.

The second thing I'd like to encourage you with is this: you've found it! You've found that secret to having it all, whatever your version of 'all' looks like. That's because I'm convinced, without a shadow of a doubt, that your true definition of 'having it all' is possible even if you don't see anything outside of you to suggest that. Everything you need is within you. I believe that every mum is herself the secret she has been looking for to create a guilt-free and harmonious situation in both work and life. I believe working mums have struggled with these issues for so long because there is no one-size-fits-all solution. Many well-intended workplace policies and initiatives have failed to successfully support mothers through these challenges because every mum has different challenges, motivations and dreams. Ask any group of mums to describe in detail their challenges and what 'having it all' means for them, and you are likely to have as many different descriptions as you have respondents, if they answer honestly.

With so many different views of the challenges facing us, and so many different ideal solutions that we all want, it's no wonder that looking outside of ourselves for 'the secret' has not been time well spent, and has instead caused us to remain overwhelmed and in reaction mode to unpredictable circumstances that seem to be getting crazier and more out of control with each year that goes by. The sad thing is, in this reaction mode the default is to worry, keep busy working other people's agendas, and consistently put ourselves last after trying to make sure everything and everyone else is okay. We often then view time just for ourselves for self-care or whatever else we want as a treat, reward or luxury that we can't usually afford. The truth, however, is that time for just yourself to keep moving towards your purpose, and what your soul is craving for you personally is something you literally can't afford to neglect, no matter how crazy life, or your to-do list, gets. In my opinion, the more hectic life is, the more necessary it is to stop going with the flow and invest some time to combat this time- and life-stealing dream killer. It does not have to take long, and it can literally be a matter of life and death, just as it was for me that night in Soho where nothing I could see in the visible realm gave me reason to believe I had any decent options. The small amount of time I invested in tackling my need to see anything to believe that a better life was possible for me very likely saved my life that night. That tiny time investment has, at the point of writing this book for you, given me back well over two decades of time living a much higher quality of life. It's been a tremendous return on investment that is available for you in your life too.

## What choice do people like you have anyway?

I appreciate that it may seem as though you have no choice but to keep going with the flow of wherever your circumstances suggest you must. That is, if you don't take the time to quiet all the noise, and to listen to that still small voice that affirms what you already know deep within, that 'this is not who you are meant to be, you are meant for so much more.' If you have settled in any way by putting off your true heart's desires in work or life due to not being able to see how it can work out, let me also echo that voice within you and repeat: 'This is not who you are meant to be, you are meant for so much more.'

Please don't waste any more time looking for a role model or anything else outside of you to show yourself that what you want is possible; I encourage you to just get going on creating your best, most fulfilling life, no matter how ambitious your goals are. While I am all for role models, and truly believe that representation matters, I also believe that a lot of the time the reason you can't see the role model you're trying to become is because you are that role model you are looking for; you are the one who has what it takes to blaze a new trail that others can follow. You are the one that others need to see to become all they can be. No matter how unqualified you may feel to be the one, it can and will be your truth if you choose to believe that wisdom that is within you telling you that you are meant for more, just as I did that night. In case you're immediately thinking, that's easy for me to say, or you don't know my personal situation and the challenges I'm facing, let me encourage you by reminding you that this hasn't worked for just me, I have helped countless clients defy the odds to become the role model they wasted years looking for.

One example of this is a brilliant woman who wasted years worrying about whether she would ever be able to make partner at her firm if she became a mum. She went on to achieve the incredible and previously impossible feat of being promoted to partner while on maternity leave through our work together. She was stunned and kept saying how much she wished she had taken the leap sooner. If she had waited for a role model to show her that she could make partner at the same time as having a baby, she very likely wouldn't have either the beautiful baby or the promotion. If she had waited to see how it would all work out, to see the whole staircase before taking the first step, as we are often tempted to, again, she very likely wouldn't have what she has now. Thankfully, she stopped needing to see it to believe it and simply got started, and she is now an inspiring role model to hundreds of women in her community who are also defying the odds to achieve great success in both their professional and personal lives. The ripple effect of this sort of impact is what I find most satisfying about my clients' success stories. I have found that what we truly want is often not just about us. There are undoubtedly many lives connected to that invisible wisdom within you asking you to believe and trust it. If you manage to find the courage to do that, there is no doubt in my mind that the visible results it will help you create will blow your and others' minds.

## How and where to invest time to overcome this dream killer

Hopefully you are now convinced, or at the very least willing to explore the notion that having it all is possible for you, however far-fetched it seems right now. If so, you might be wondering how exactly you get started. Luckily, the answer is simple: you make a firm decision to have it all – whatever that means to you person- ally – and to create the most amazing version of both your personal and professional lives that you can see within you, no matter what you currently see happening, or not happening, outside of you. You can decide that you are no longer available to spend and waste your time reacting to overwhelming circumstances and situations that just make you feel worried, exhausted, frustrated and further away from the life you hoped to be living by now. You can truly decide by cutting off all other options – no plan B!

Again, in case you are one of the women who reads this and thinks that's impossible for you, given all that you're dealing with, let me say this: you're right, I don't know your personal situation, and I'm definitely not trying to gaslight you or belittle your lived experience either. My heart truly goes out to you – I wouldn't be investing the time to write this book if it didn't. I totally get that being a mum is hard work – really hard work at times, especially if your kids are at a challenging development stage. Actually, come to think of it, every stage of raising a child has its own crazy challenges, and just when you think you have things figured out, they hit the next one. Perhaps you are raising a child with special needs, or one of the many other situations that can make things cry-into-your-pillow tough.

All that said, when we spend life reacting to or worrying about these challenges, and writing never-ending to-do lists based on them, we are setting ourselves up for the life of our nightmares rather than the life of our dreams that we really want to be living. Here's the truth, Mama: your dream life in which you take amazing care of yourself, your family and your to-dos doesn't happen by default as you react to what you see in life – you have to deliberately create it from the unseen realm.

You achieve that by doing what I like to think of as taking your eyes off the peanuts and focusing on the endless possibilities instead. Here's what I mean by that: no matter how chaotic or unpredictable things look in your life right now, there are endless possibilities available to you in the unseen realm right at this very second. This is not just me being the eternal optimist that I am, but an actual scientific fact. In physics, everything you can see is made up of tiny atoms – from the things that make up the planet, like mountains and stars, to us human beings and even the things we own like this book you are reading right now – literally all of it is made up of atoms; bundles of teeny tiny atoms are the building blocks of our world. Scientists have also found that if you look closely at an atom, the nucleus that is at the centre of the atom, and the only part of the atom that you can see, is way less than 1 per cent of the size of the full atom. Most of the atom is made up of stuff that you can't see; so if you imagine that the part of the atom you can see is the size of a peanut, the actual size of the atom is about the size of a massive sports stadium!

Think about that for a second – atoms, which are the building blocks of every single thing you can see right now, are almost entirely invisible! I don't know about you, but I found it totally mind-blowing when I first heard that, and even more mind-blowing when I got curious about the endless possibilities in that vast invisible realm and started to apply my findings to my life as a mother. This helped me to understand that, in any moment, regardless of what our lives look like, there are infinite possibilities. Stop and look around you right now and let that idea sink in. There are infinite possibilities beyond worrying about how your kids fit in with your own personal dreams and goals; infinite possibilities beyond feeling bad about the house being nowhere near as clean as you'd like; infinite possibilities beyond getting frustrated at the partner that is nowhere near as helpful as you would like them to be around said house; infinite possibilities beyond feeling like the worst mum ever because you screamed at everyone earlier; infinite possibilities beyond all of it. However, if you keep focusing on and reacting to these peanuts that you can see, you'll never grasp and begin to create what's possible that you can't yet see with your naked eyes.

To illustrate this, let me take you back to my story where I accidently discovered this strategy again. As I stood there, a total mess, face to face with that pimp, feeling so ashamed, terrified and alone, there was nothing in the visible realm to suggest I had any other options but to keep digging past rock bottom to work for him. But when I heard that voice in my head, I took my eyes off the peanuts of the nightmare of a life I had created for myself and reached for possibilities that have since proved to go far beyond anything I could have even imagined in that petrifying moment.

The same is available to you right now: a life far beyond anything you could ever imagine in this very moment – no matter what it looks or feels like for you right now. I hope things are not as desperate and scary for you in that moment as they were for me, but even if they are worse, there is always hope when you decide to believe the truth that anything is possible! You can create a life beyond your wildest dreams. Whether you got to this place through your own bad choices like I did, or you find yourself here through no fault of your own, the possibilities are endless when you decide to believe and go for it. We often hear people say the phrase, 'seeing is believing,' but the actual truth is that believing is seeing. Every witty invention, every beautiful work of art, every delicious meal, everything exists because someone somewhere once believed it was possible first, and then went on to create it for others to see and benefit from. Will you believe me when I say that you too are meant for so much more, so that you can create and finally see it? If so, I'd love for you to deal with this dream killer of needing to see it to believe it right now and decide that you will begin to create your 'more' with me as we continue through this book.

Decide to go for the 'more' you know deep down that you are meant for! Jump into it feeling afraid if you have to. Do it without having to have all the answers. Do it without a role model if there isn't one available, trusting that you will figure it out as you go. It might be daunting to move ahead in the absence of role models that look like you to show you what you want is possible, but the truth is that the world you and I were born into no longer exists – so much has changed and continues to change rapidly. With so much uncertainty and continuous change in what we see with our eyes, we could all benefit from getting better at trusting and following the powerful wisdom within us, as much, if not more, than we look externally for permission and proof. So, if you have the desire within you to continue progressing with your career while your family grows, it's very likely that it's possible and meant for you even if you can't see how right now. Where there is a will there is a way, as the old adage goes. You don't need to waste any more time worrying what might happen, or putting your goals and dreams last. Decide that you'll go for it all and figure it out as you go. And I do mean truly decide – which is to say, you need to cut off all other options and go for this like your life depends on it, because it does.

When I made a firm decision to turn my life around in Soho on that night those decades ago, there was no going back, and I invite you to be that firm in your decision today. I wish I could tell you that once you make a firm decision everything will fall into place and work out. As we have already said, life can be challenging, intense and uncertain. It's extremely easy to default back to reacting to what you see with your eyes, especially if you have spent your whole life doing so, rather than being guided by your internal wisdom, which is why I recommend you take some time each day to tap into the infinite possibilities in the unseen realm to strengthen your belief that what you want is possible even if you can't yet see it, and to get guidance. The good news is that, as you work on adding the weekly and daily habits we touched on in the last chapter into your life, you'll already be doing this. You might recall the daily habits included using tools such as meditation, visualisation and journaling to transcend the limitations and frustrations that may currently exist in your life and get clarity on your 'must-do' items. The more you do this, and follow through on the wisdom you get, the more you too will begin to pull from the unseen realm to create the impossible in your life. This is a non-negotiable part of every single day for me, and a powerful part of my morning routine. It is usually just a few minutes of time invested, which brings a vast return in terms of time and quality of life improvements, thanks to the insights I receive and implement from it.

## Creation exercise

With that, I want to lead you into a brief creation exercise to help you rise above the peanuts in your life and anchor yourself in the decision to create your best possible life, starting today. I'd love for you to imagine and picture this scenario as vividly as possible in your mind. The clearer the pictures you can see as we go through this exercise, the better. If using a pen and paper helps you envision and imagine better feel free to use them.

Your phone rings and it's me on the line, inviting you to a no-expense-spared, life-changing trip I have arranged for you. I add that I will reveal more about the destination on the way.

I sense some hesitation and questions swirling in your mind, so I also add that it's just one quick flight away and, don't worry, I've made sure that your work, family, or anything else you might be worried about will be just fine in your absence.

You think to yourself, it sure would be nice to have a bit of a break from it all for a little while, so you agree to it and jump in the taxi I sent to bring you to the airport. You're met there by airline staff who greet you warmly, check you in, then lead you through security to wait for boarding in luxury in the lounge. After enjoying a delicious snack and beverage of choice there, you are invited to board the flight and are led into first class onboard. You are treated like the queen you are every step of the way. Any Champagne? You decide. I booked a window seat for you, and as we take off, I invite you to imagine all the fears, cares and worries that you have about life drifting away and becoming smaller and less significant, just like the things on Earth appear the higher we rise.

When we get to the cruising altitude of 37,000 feet, again I prompt you to look out of the window and reflect on how small things down there look from up here. Everything that you were worried and frustrated about even just an hour ago look like peanuts from this high up, right? You agree with me, then ask the obvious question: 'But where are we going?' To which I reply, that it is completely up to you. You get to decide.

To help you decide, I invite you to take a few moments to honestly answer these questions right now. You can write in a journal if it helps.

### How or where in my life am I settling for less than I dreamt of for my future? And why?

It may be tempting to skip this introspection and just keep reading, but I urge you not to. Your life- and destiny-altering break-through could lie right here – in your truthful answers. As ancient wisdom states, the truth will set you free. From this 37,000-foot view of your life, reflect on how and why you are settling.

For me as a new mum, I was settling everywhere, never taking a moment just for myself because I believed that's what good mums have to do – sacrifice so their kids can succeed, even if that made them miserable. What's your version? When you have it, I'd love for you to ask yourself this next question:

### What will life look like for me and my family if I do nothing and keep living this way?

Again, answer as truthfully as you can.

In my case, I knew that I did not want to live anything less than the best possible life for myself. However, as I wanted to be a good mum and please everyone, I was willing to sacrifice what I wanted for myself to look after my family and everything else first, even if it left me feeling overwhelmed, unfulfilled and even resentful at times. That was until I learnt about social learning theory, which was developed by the psychologist Albert Bandura in 1977. Social learning theory suggests that our kids learn how to behave by watching and copying others, especially us, their parents. So, even though I was hoping to help my kids succeed in life with all my sacrificing, I was actually setting them up to become just like I was later in life: overwhelmed, unfulfilled and resentful! That's when I decided something had to change. No turning back.

What about you? What will life look like for you and your family if you do nothing and keep living this way? Are you happy with the picture you see ahead if life continues as it is? If so, and you are willing for your kids to grow up approaching life like you do, and feeling how you do about it now, I can set the destination of our flight back to exactly where you are coming from.

There is no judgement if this is your decision, by the way – as I said before, I get that the pressure coming against us from all directions, including society, can be intense. It's exhausting just to think about it sometimes, so I get that not everyone is ready to deal with that level of opposition and tackle the weight of everyone's expectations. If that's you, it's totally fine and your choice to make. If, however, you want something more than you are currently living, for both you and your children, I will be setting your destination to 'so much more'.

To mark this moment, I would love for you to say this out loud right now:

***I am meant for so much more, and I make my decision to go for that, no matter what; there will be no turning back.***

I mean that, by the way. Before you continue reading, literally say that line out loud, as there is so much power in the words we say.

*I am meant for so much more, and I make my decision to go for that, no matter what; there will be no turning back.*

Now you've made this decision, as you come back down to earth and your daily life, I invite you to commit to your non-negotiable daily habits. Any time you are tempted to think you can't have it all because you can't be what you can't see, I want you to remember that even if you can't see it with your eyes, you can be it if you see it with your heart. Do what you can daily to believe with all your heart what you want is possible, and you will see, as I and countless of my clients have, that believing is indeed seeing. Best of all, as you commit to continuously creating the impossible in this way, like us, you will make your family your reason for living your best possible life, instead of your excuse for not doing so. Deal with this dream killer once and for all by deciding today to believe the dream inside of you is possible, no matter what you see outside of you. The next generation is relying on you to decide. The next generation is relying on you to take action. The next generation is relying on you, Mama.

## Key takeaways

- If you feel like you have no choice but to settle for less than the life you know deep down that you are meant for, chances are you are being robbed of time and quality of life by the dream killer of needing to see it to believe it.
- Your true definition of 'having it all' is possible, even if you don't see anything outside of you to suggest that. Everything you need to get started is within you.

- When we spend life reacting to or worrying about our visible challenges, and writing never-ending to-do lists based on them, we are setting ourselves up for the life of our nightmares, rather than the life of our dreams.

- Your dream life in which you take amazing care of yourself, your family and your to-dos doesn't happen by default as you react to what you see in life; you have to deliberately create it from the unseen realm. You achieve that by taking your eyes off the peanuts and focusing on the endless possibilities in the unseen realm instead.

- We often hear people say 'seeing is believing', but the actual truth is that believing is seeing.

- Decide to go for the 'more' you know deep down that you are meant for! Do it afraid, if you have to. Do it without having to have all the answers, or even a role model, trusting that you will figure it out as you go.

- What you want deep down is usually about much more than just you. Others' destinies are often tied to yours, and once you blaze your unique trail, what was impossible now becomes possible for others. Perhaps most importantly, your kids are watching and will do what they see you doing. You owe it to yourself and them to create and live a life so incredible that you would be happy to see them emulate it.

# Chapter 3: Life Crises!

I arrived at the University of Wales Bangor in September 2000 to start my degree in Banking and Finance. Apart from the occasional fear that someone would find out about me and my far-from-normal past, it was an incredible experience. I felt like I had a fresh start at life with the beginning of the new millennium. Instead of the rejection I feared, I was warmly accepted.

I was so fortunate and blessed to encounter great friends and incredible staff and a faculty that liked and believed in me. Gradually, I managed to break free of so many of the crazy habits that had been normal in my life thus far and began to thrive again.

The amazing professors and faculty had such a profound impact on me; one of the team told me he saw a great future ahead for me, and he even went above and beyond what was required to recommend me for an incredible internship to start me on the way towards it. Based on his recommendations, I was accepted for an amazing year-long internship at an international bank in Chester between the second and final years of my degree.

The internship year went phenomenally, and I secured a full-time job offer with the bank for after graduation before even starting my final year at university. By the time I got to my final year, I'd heard over and over from my supportive teachers that, based on my performance over the years, I had the potential to graduate with first-class honours – the very best grade you can get. They said it would take a lot of hard work in the final year, but they believed I could do it. That was music to my ears, so I made that my vision for graduation. My 'why' was simple and extremely motivating to me; graduating with top grades would make up for the big mess I had made of my life in the past, so I could really start afresh. I could make my family feel pride instead of shame.

As you can imagine, such encouragement, support and progress would be phenomenal for any student, but for me, who was once told I'd amount to nothing, it was more phenomenal than I can find the words to describe here. I was starting to see the 'more' that I had heard that little voice telling me I was meant for that night in Soho, and I was so grateful that I'd trusted that internal wisdom, even when there was nothing that I could see to support it in the visible realm.

In December of that final year of university, my family planned a big trip back to Nawfia, in Anambra state in the east of Nigeria where my family is from, for Christmas and then a traditional event. Due to my university commitments, I could not travel to Nigeria until right before the Christmas festivities, so my parents and siblings went ahead to help organise the celebrations. The plan was for me to fly into Lagos in the southwest of Nigeria when I was done with university stuff, then meet up with two of our family friends, Peter and Justus, before heading east together to meet everyone else. I wanted to stay on track for my first-class honours result in my degree, so I intended to carve out some time immediately after the celebrations to study for my exams and thesis proposal submission, which were both due in January. I was so excited for this perfect plan – and a trip of a lifetime! Little did I know as I boarded the flight to Nigeria that I was embarking on a crisis-ridden nightmare journey from hell.

Things started off great; I was happy to meet my family friends when I landed at Lagos airport. I also gladly welcomed the familiar hustle and bustle of Lagos, the city of my birth and early childhood days. It felt amazing to be back that first day. However, as we began to make plans to drive east the next day for the festivities, I started to get a heavy sense of foreboding. You know that feeling you get in your gut that tries to warn you that something bad is going to happen? I had that the whole day but I just ignored it, too scared about what I would find if I investigated it. After a strange day, mostly spent desperately avoiding entertaining my thoughts, I had a restless night's sleep before waking up that Christmas Eve ready to set off for the journey east with my friends. The journey should have taken seven hours maximum by car, but instead it took more than ten times that, and it involved an endless stream of catastrophic events that had us fearing for our safety and lives almost the entire time. The first was a near-fatal car accident when the front left tyre of our car flew off while we were driving on the motorway, which caused the car to spin rapidly out of control and zigzag across lanes of speeding traffic to the side of the road.

It was miracle that we ended up there unharmed. The screaming locals who ran to our wreck of a car, now complete with smoke pouring out of the engine, said they were surprised to find anyone alive inside, based on what they watched happen to the car after the tyre flew off.

Just as we were trying to get over the shock and figure out what to do next, we were totally taken advantage of by a group of local thieves where we had broken down – in Ore, in Ondo state.

There was no equivalent of the roadside assistance that I had for my car back in the UK, which gave me the option of someone to call in the event of a breakdown or accident. We were still well over two hundred kilometres from our destination, and too far from our starting point in Lagos to call for help, so we were at the mercy of whoever showed up; all this while running out of food, water and phone battery life, in the middle of nowhere, under the boiling-hot Nigerian sun.

The thieves must have spotted us stranded there for the two hours that we were on the side of the road trying to figure out a solution, so one of them came over, pretending to help us, and offered to tow our vehicle into the nearest town, to his friends who were mechanics. He assured us that they would be able to help us, and that we would be on our way to our destination in no time. We were so grateful and couldn't thank him enough. He towed us there, and his friends got to work on the engine.

Their 'work' took over six hours and involved totally dismantling the engine while speaking among themselves in their native language, which we didn't understand, and ignoring any questions that we had. When it seemed every single part of the engine was on the ground, the lead mechanic, a shirtless, dirty-looking, pot-bellied man finally spoke up in English and said he had basically finished all he was going to do, and if we wanted him to complete the work so we could leave safely, we would have to give him pretty much all the money we had. In reality, the work should have cost a tiny fraction of what he was demanding, but they knew that we had no choice; it had started to get dark on these roads that are notorious for being treacherous to travellers even in the daytime. There were no streetlights, we had no knowledge of the local language that everyone was speaking (Nigeria has hundreds), no working vehicle and no GPS. This was before the days of the internet at your fingertips through your phone; we were totally at their mercy. Every once in a while, that awful man would also look at me from head to toe with a sleazy smile on his face, which made us worry that I was in grave danger of being sexually assaulted if we stayed there much longer. The fear and disgust combined made me feel like running to find somewhere to throw up, but I didn't dare move in case it drew more attention to myself.

Peter, whose car it was, was furious, but as we were totally outnumbered and clearly in serious danger, he had to give in. He felt responsible for getting us to our destination safely, and so he handed over the vast majority of the funds we had on us to the thieving workmen. The men carried on fixing the car for another two hours before they finally said it was done. We were relieved to hear the engine start and overjoyed to be safely on our way a few minutes after. It had been a long, horrific day and experience, but at least we were all physically fine and could continue our journey. Our relief, however, was short-lived.

As we were trying to decide whether to continue on the journey east or find somewhere to spend the night and continue on in the morning, a loud explosion from the engine decided for us. The bodge job those thieves did barely got us ten kilometres down the road from their garage before something in the engine exploded, causing the car to gradually slow to a complete halt, and more smoke to come out of the engine than last time. This was becoming quite the living nightmare. Thankfully, this latest catastrophe happened just outside a service station, so we were able to push the car in there to spend the night.

As you can imagine, there was little sleep, a lot of stress, and much racking of our brains to see how we could get the few naira we were left with to stretch far enough to get food and all three of us to our destination, which was still over two hundred kilometres away. We called our families and informed them of the situation, and tried not to let their worried tones impact us too much. We had all heard countless stories of armed robberies on these same roads in broad daylight, so the thought that we would have to spend the night in the car out in the open was an alarming one for us. There was nothing anyone could do about it though, and as the battery on the last phone still on was nearly dead, we had to end the call to save what we could of that.

My dad assured us that the entire family was praying for our safe arrival early the next day, Christmas morning. I thought, if only we can figure this out and get there early in the day so we can spend some of Christmas with our families, then perhaps this whole thing would not be so bad. As I looked up at the Ondo night sky, wishing and hoping, I thought for a moment about my life, friends and tutors at Bangor University. I wondered how they would be waking up on Christmas morning. I thought about kids around the world hoping that Santa Claus would visit this Christmas Eve night with gifts. That's not something we did in Nigeria growing up, so I always found the Santa thing that parents do so funny and fascinating when I learnt about it after my family moved to the UK when I was eleven. Christmas traditions definitely felt like a world away now that we were stuck sleeping in a broken-down vehicle, hoping and praying to make it into Christmas morning without attracting the attention of any more thieves.

I thought of my vision to graduate with first-class honours. Was it still possible? Perhaps...?

*We'll get there tomorrow, have our Christmas celebrations and other events, then I can travel back, put all this behind me, and study to make it happen.* I was lost in my thoughts when Peter interrupted and advised me and Justus to get some sleep – he would stay up to keep watch. Around 4am, I finally drifted off into a light, troubled sleep with my head against the window in the back seat of the car. Less than an hour later, I was woken up by the light from the rising sun, and unfamiliar sounds. For a minute, I was confused, wondering where I was, then the events of the previous day came flooding back to me. My heart sank. This was not how I imagined waking up at Christmas time.

I looked over at Peter, who looked exhausted. He said he had figured it out; we would get the relatively inexpensive Danfo buses from here to our destination. We would need to make a few changes as there were no direct buses, but we could get there eventually. I was relieved – we were safe, and we had a plan. The thing with these relatively cheap, mass-transit Danfo buses, however, is that you have very little say in the schedule. The drivers usually wait for enough passengers to board and pay fares to make it worth their while to start the journey, so it was well into the afternoon on Christmas Day before we set off, and it ended up taking several bus changes and two more days to get to my hometown of Nawfia, during which we slept on the streets at night again.

We finally arrived a few short hours before one of the main traditional celebrations was scheduled to take place. Seeing my family and everything set up for the event caused me to burst into tears. I cried because I had been almost certain that I would never see them again as we went through hell trying to get there. I cried because of the love they had clearly poured into all the preparations – it looked lovely. After quick greetings to everyone, I was rushed to eat and get ready so we could stay on schedule with the start of the event.

I took one look in the mirror – I looked like I had been dragged through a hedge backwards after that hellish journey. As I got dressed, I heard guests already beginning to arrive for the event. The combined sound of their conversations and sporadic laughter sounded almost musical. I suddenly realised I hadn't smiled or laughed for a very long time and I was looking forward to having reason to once again do so at the party. I came out of the room, took a deep breath, and headed to the front compound of the house where the party canopies were set up. There were a lot of people already gathered there by that time, and as I looked around, the first familiar face I saw was my dad's. I noticed immediately that he didn't look right, almost like he had been crying. I figured that the stress of the last three days must have been so much to bear emotionally, with us on the road in terrible danger, so I didn't say anything.

Hundreds of people continued to arrive, and it ended up being a colourful and lively event that everyone seemed to enjoy – except my dad. Several of my chance glances in his direction caught him still looking teary eyed and like he was a million miles away, alone in his thoughts in the midst of the crowd. I wondered why; it seemed strange that he would still be so emotional hours after we had arrived safely. With all the guests and activity, I didn't get the chance to speak to him before going to bed that night. I was extremely concerned, but I fell asleep almost as soon as my head hit the pillow. I was overwhelmed with gratitude to be sleeping in an actual bed again for the first time in days.

When I woke up the next morning, I quickly found out what the issue was with my dad. One of the people in the village informed me that his mother, my paternal grandmother, had passed away due to illness while we were stuck on the road. So my father had that to contend with, in addition to our crisis. That explained his tears, and so much else about how he was acting. He did not want to ruin the event that had been planned for months, so he kept it to himself, bless him. The pain of my own grief quickly engulfed me, and I sobbed uncontrollably for much of that day, and the rest of the trip. The time and energy I had planned to use for university work was spent grieving and being there for my dad.

When I finally got back to Bangor after the holiday from hell, I felt so disconnected from my university work and vision of achieving a first, given all I had been through. I had regular flashbacks and nightmares of the traumatic experiences from my trip, but I pushed through them to catch up and turn in the next major assignment. This was a proposal for my dissertation that I managed to submit to my teaching supervisor late on a Thursday afternoon. I was proud to have done this well in advance of the Monday deadline, so I could focus on catching up on revision for exams in a few days.

I was surprised to receive a message the next day saying my thesis supervisor wanted to see me. I walked into his office expecting to be greeted by his usual smiley and encouraging face, but instead he looked annoyed and disappointed. He then proceeded to tell me in no uncertain terms that, based on what I had submitted for my proposal, achieving a first-class honours would be practically impossible, and I'd be lucky to even pass my degree, as the dissertation is such a major proportion of one's overall mark.

Before I could explain about the hell I had been through over the Christmas break that caused the quality of my work to suffer, he went on to list several major issues with the proposal, including lack of adequate research, structure and a basic application of common sense. He ended with a damning summary: 'The reason we give so much time to complete this over the holidays is because it needs it. There is weeks' worth of work to do to make this even basic standard, never mind first-class honours standard. You have until the Monday deadline if you want to resubmit something, however if you choose not to, I am not sure I can even pass this.'

I left his office shell-shocked, holding back the tears from rolling down my face. Some friends saw and called out, asking me if I was okay, but I felt so embarrassed and ran past them, all the way back to my small room on Glanrafon Hill where I could cry my eyes out in peace. With all that he had told me was wrong with my thesis, there was no way I could fix this! He had made clear that to achieve what was necessary would take weeks of work; how on earth could I possibly do that with only a weekend? On top of all that, there were the exams that I also needed to get ready for – I'd planned to spend my weekend revising. I had no idea what to do, but I suddenly realised that I had been holding my breath for a while, so I stopped, took a deep long breath in, and then breathed out slowly. It felt good, so I did it again, and again, and again. The deep breaths helped to calm me down and gave me a key shift in perspective.

My question of 'What can I even achieve in a weekend?' slowly changed to 'What have you achieved in a weekend in the past?' There was so much that I could think about. In a weekend, I had totally changed the trajectory of my life when I moved from London to Bangor, far away from the friends and influences that were keeping me stuck in a lifestyle that no longer served me. In a weekend, I had studied enough to score the highest marks the tutors had seen during the last exam cycle. In a weekend, I fixed an issue that the company where I'd spent my internship had been facing for a long time. They were so impressed that they issued me the company's Above and Beyond Award – this was the first time this prestigious award had ever been given to an intern. Reflecting on these past wins made me realise that I could do a lot in a weekend to get me back on track to my vision of scoring top marks.

Feeling empowered, and sensing a tiny spark of hope, I sat in silence for a moment, reflecting on what it would take to write a first-class proposal in a weekend. With that, I felt the urge to grab a pen and paper, and began to write. First, I made notes from my conversation with my supervisor, focusing purely on the ton of constructive feedback and advice he had given me, resisting the temptation to dwell on some of the other comments that I had been taking personally. From those, I structured what I believed a first-class proposal would look like. I didn't have all that I needed to pull it off, but I got the sense that I was meant to start writing up what I did have. Three hours later, I had several pages done and it was looking great. The whole thing was looking more doable, but there was the small issue of the weeks' worth of work that I didn't have time for. So, once again, I got quiet and asked myself: 'How can I do the best job of this in the time I have?' I felt compelled to reach out to a few of my fellow students for help; one to help me with the actual work gathering journal papers to research and include in my proposal, and the others to help with food and so on. I was clearly going to have to pull a couple of all-nighters to be in with a chance of doing this properly.

They graciously agreed to help, and I got to work. As I worked, I could see my vision gradually becoming possible again. Reconnecting to that, and to my 'why' of wanting to make my parents feel pride instead of shame, was also powerful. This gave me more alertness than any cup of coffee ever could as I read and wrote day and night throughout that weekend. Any time I felt weak, I would meditate on empowering thoughts that gave me strength to continue, including one I had read recently: 'I can do anything that I set my mind to.' Staying focused on my vision, why, and pushing through, led to me resubmitting a first-class proposal that went on to become an award-winning dissertation. That sleep-deprived weekend was so worth it! I was awarded the university's Jack Revell Prize, which is given to the student with the best and highest-scoring banking and finance dissertation. I will be forever grateful to my thesis supervisor for believing in me enough to give his candid, albeit initially upsetting, feedback. It was a gamechanger! Using the same sort of approach, I also went on to ace my exams and graduate at the top of the class with first-class honours, despite so many other things threatening to derail me from achieving my vision.

I don't think I have adequate words to describe how it felt as I walked across the graduation stage, grinning as wide as a Cheshire cat to receive my award and degree with my parents, siblings, friends and faculty clapping with pride. Happy tears rolled down my cheeks as I realised that I was proud of myself too; so proud to have achieved the impossible, and to now feel like I had the world as my oyster as a first-class honours graduate.

I analysed this experience to understand what it was that kept me on track to success in the face of such chaos and dream-killing crises to help you do the same as you encounter crises in your life.

## Overcoming this dream killer

I wish I could tell you that it's smooth sailing and a peaceful flight to your vision of 'having it all' once you make a firm decision to go for it, but as we all know, and as you saw in my story – life happens. For all of us, at some point, we encounter the equivalent of turbulence on a flight when a crisis shows up unexpectedly and completely knocks the wind out of our sails, making us feel powerless. Since that holiday from hell, I have seen many more crises pop up and attempt to derail me from creating the life I dream of – and I've seen my clients experience it too. Depending on their severity, crises can be one of the most effective dream killers, because we often don't see them coming and they typically feel all-consuming. The death of a loved one just before a major event being planned, dealing with a seriously ill child alongside significant work commitments, and even extreme situations such as war breaking out in the country are just some examples of the numerous major crises that I have helped women to successfully navigate.

When an unexpected crisis hits us, whether big or small, we can very quickly go from feeling ready to take on the world and create our vision, to feeling like the world has gone totally crazy, and that the only thing left to do is to crawl under our pillow and hide until it regains sanity. If you are facing any kind of crisis, you might be wondering what to do instead.

Is it even possible to avoid diverting time from focusing on your own goals and ambitions when you are in the middle of a full-on crisis that you cannot control or predict, especially with kids and other loved ones to think about and care for? How can you even dare to continue thinking about your vision of having it all, never mind continuing to create it, when you feel like the only thing you have time for right now is your urgent and important role of fire-fighter, a role for which you've never had training! I totally get it if you are thinking any of that – I probably would be too if I was reading rather than writing this. However, my life experiences and those of my clients have taught me that there is a more empowered and time-efficient way to handle even the most unexpected, unpredictable and unprecedented crisis.

While we may not be able to control what is happening during a crisis, we can always control how we respond to it – and how we respond really does make all the difference. The right response can make a crisis, and the chaos it brings with it, compensate you, in my experience. For example, one of my clients suddenly found herself in an unimaginable situation when conflict broke out in her home country. Through our work together, she was able to move her children and entire extended family to a new country, in which she managed to secure a new job that was even a step up on her career path, and resettle her family's life into a new routine that suits them.

The key for her, for me, for you and for anyone else who wants to create the impossible in their moments of crisis, is to become intentional about how we use our time. Try to not allow this dream killer to cause you to just waste or spend all your time reacting to the visible effects of the crisis. You must become a deliberate investor of your time to succeed in times of crisis. Before I go into exactly how you do that, I want to highlight an important distinction that you must make to successfully navigate the crisis you are facing.

There may be situations where the best use of all your time is to react and respond to what you see, such as in times of true emergency, where you or someone else is in danger, or in desperate need of immediate assistance – like the grave danger I found myself in during my trip to Nigeria. In such times of emergency crisis, your time is best invested in dealing with what you can see in order to get to the most favourable outcome possible.

Then there are other types of crises – the non-life-threatening or dangerous kind – which are disruptive because they threaten your ability to fulfil the vision of having it all that you set for yourself, like when I was safely back from my trip and had the disastrous meeting with my supervising professor. In these latter types of crises, which will be my focus for the rest of this chapter, if you skilfully invest your time, you too can create the most incredible outcome for yourself and your family against all odds.

So, how exactly do you do that? I'm glad you asked.

## The six-step CRISIS success plan

When facing a crisis or dealing with things out of your control that make your already ambitious vision look totally crazy under the circumstances, I recommend you respond by implementing the six-step CRISIS success plan I have developed. CRISIS is an acronym that will hopefully make the six steps that form this plan easier for you to remember when you need it. It will help you rise above the turbulence you encountered to stay on track to your vision of 'so much more'.

## C: Cut out all the noise

When you find yourself in turbulent times, start with the first step, C of CRISIS, which stands for **Cut out all the noise** – that is, the noise that comes from other people, the news, and so on. This will allow you to tap into and access your own powerful wisdom. Try not to give in to the incredibly tempting tendency to make knee-jerk reactions or to immediately run to other people to get their input and opinion. In fact, I strongly urge you not to do that.

After that disastrous thesis proposal meeting with my supervising professor, I had the perfect opportunity to stop and talk to my friends who called out to me as I ran back to my room, cry on their shoulders and get their sympathy and opinions. While it might have felt so good to do that – to vent and share my frustrations for a minute – with hindsight I can see with crystal clarity that taking that simple, seemingly helpful step would have robbed me of my award-winning result. I can say that with confidence, because no matter what was said, there is no way that conversation would have set me up to create the massive turnaround that I needed to pull off that weekend.

Those friends were good, lovely people who meant well, but they were very different from me in terms of their own goals and the ways they approached life. They did not have the same challenging past that I had had, or the desperate need and drive to make things right that I did. As a result, their advice in that moment may have been great advice for them, but not necessarily for me. It would have been filtered through their own past experiences, future ambitions, their current opinions of the supervising professor and so much more, none of which had any relevance to me and my life's purpose and journey.

Often when crisis hits our lives we immediately run to others and effectively waste time, giving our power away by asking for and following advice that has been filtered through their own situations, both past and present, as well as their future hopes, all of which can often have little to no relevance to us personally, or to where our purpose wants to lead us. This then leads to us wasting even more time implementing solutions that would be their idea of success and not ours – and that kind of success is rarely fulfilling.

I urge you to take back your power in these situations by initially cutting out all the noise in a crisis, and prioritising some time alone, so you can begin to access the amazing wisdom within you that is more likely to work for you personally. I am by no means implying that you are to do everything on your own and never ask for help; on the contrary, I am a big believer in asking for help, and lots of it too, but this must be done in the right emotional state, at the right time, and from the right people.

## R: Remember past successes and Refocus on your vision

The next step in the CRISIS success plan is two for the price of one: the R that will help you get into the right emotional state from which to ask for help or anything else you need; an inspired, empowered state. You get to that state by **Remembering past successes** and **Refocusing on your vision**.

Often, when we are in the middle of a crisis it feels like we will never get through it; that we might as well give up. The truth is that no matter who you are, the chances are you have overcome something in your past. There might have been things that once looked impossible to overcome, but you somehow did. In this new crisis, it is so helpful to remember those past successes, and to encourage yourself with the knowledge that this too shall pass, and that you have what it takes to get through it. Once you've done this, now is a great time to refocus on your vision, remembering that this crisis and all you can see is less than 1 per cent of what actually is. It's just peanuts compared to the infinite possibilities available to you right now in the invisible realm. If it helps, you can take a few moments to meditate on your vision to the point where you believe it is still possible for you to achieve and you are ready to start figuring out the next steps. This is such a powerful practice for me any time crisis starts to overwhelm me. I take time to remember how resourceful I have been in the past with solving pressing challenges. This, and meditating on my vision, brings back peace, calm and openness to the infinite possibilities that are available.

## I: Inquire intelligently about your next steps

Once you are reconnected to your vision and feeling empowered, it is the right time for the next step in the CRISIS success plan, which is I: *Inquire intelligently about your next steps*. You do this by tapping into your powerful internal wisdom. This does not have to be mysterious or difficult, it can be as simple as asking great questions of yourself, by which I mean questions that you actually want to know the answer to. When you receive and implement the answers to these questions, the answers will move you closer to realising your vision.

Don't fall into the mistake that so many of us do when facing a crisis and ask questions like, 'What's wrong with me?' or, 'What's wrong with you?' to our partner or kids. In those moments, we don't really want to know what's wrong with anyone; rather, we want a solution to the crisis we're facing. The truth is that we get what we focus on, so if we focus on questions such as this, or others that don't really help our situation, that's what we will get. So, in a crisis, inquire about your next steps with great questions that connect you to intelligent answers that can help move you towards your vision.

This step has been so powerful for me as a mum and during many times of crisis before that. One memorable occasion was just before marrying my amazing husband Nnamdi in 2013. One week before our wedding, a crisis of epic proportions hit when my soon-to-be father-in-law suddenly passed away from a brief and unexpected illness. It was such a painful and confusing time for the family as we grieved and wondered what to do about our wedding. One of a few great questions that helped us move forward was asking, 'What would our dear dad Rufus have wanted?' This led us to recall that when Rufus realised that he might not survive his illness, he was very clear that no matter what happened to him, the wedding must go on. That simple dying wish gave us all the supernatural strength we needed to get through that final week of preparations and have the wedding.

It's honestly one of the hardest things I have ever walked through, but it was like Papa Rufus was somehow with us every step of the way, especially during the many times it got tough coping with the sadness. After Nnamdi and I exchanged vows in the church, we sang what had been his dad's favourite hymn, 'How Great Thou Art'. There was truly something almost otherworldly about that experience. As I looked out at the over five hundred guests from fifty-five different nations singing, I could see many with tears in their eyes as mine also filled up. It was as though Rufus somehow connected with us during that song. It was beautiful, peaceful and powerful.

Inquiring intelligently about our next steps with great questions every step of the way helped us to find courage, peace, power and beauty during one of the most painful and difficult crises we have ever faced. I believe it can do the same for you.

## S: Seek input from carefully selected sources

Step number four in the CRISIS success plan is S: ***Seek input from carefully selected sources***. After you have inquired about your next steps, it's time to get input and help from others. I can't emphasise the 'carefully selected sources' part enough. This is so crucial to your success. You want to make sure that whomever or whatever you seek input from is in support of your vision.

For example, I worked with a woman who was trying to overcome fear and keep moving forward with her vision during a time of crisis after an unexpected and fatal attack, resulting in hundreds of deaths, triggered widespread panic in her nation. A powerful approach for her was to deliberately limit news intake significantly, because excessive amounts of it, especially first thing in the morning, put her in a paralysing state of fear, consuming her time and halting her progress. She watched just enough news to understand what was happening, and to learn what she absolutely needed to know to stay safe, to keep others safe and to effectively fulfil her role as a business leader. Quite importantly, between us we agreed she would only watch such absolutely necessary news after she had completed step 2, R in the CRISIS success plan, in which she remembered past successes and refocused on her vision through an empowering meditation. She was then able to extract necessary insights from the news, and with the help of a handful of trusted advisers she could keep moving towards her goals. This worked wonderfully for her and her family. No matter the crisis you are facing, the same rules apply: you should thoroughly vet who or what you let into your life.

In the course of doing this work for many years, one of the things that pains me so much is the incredible amount of judgement that we deal with as mothers, which makes us feel like we are failing as mums and, quite frankly, in everything else too. Sadly, a lot of the time this judgement comes from other women. It's important to bear in mind that not every woman or mum will agree with your vision, and that's okay; just be incredibly selective about who you share with and seek input from, especially during times of crisis. The last thing you need is judgement that makes you wobble in your conviction of what you want. Stick with those who you are sure support you and your vision – and leave out anyone that doesn't.

After my upsetting conversation with my thesis supervisor when dealing with the crisis I faced at university, though I was tempted to be annoyed and upset, I had to get over myself and realise that he was actually trying to help me. The reason he acted that way was because he actually cared a great deal about my results and wanted me to succeed. This is what led me to analyse everything he had said to me so I could extract what I needed to do in order to reach that success, while doing my best to move past the parts of the conversation that upset me.

I have had to take a similar approach with things like work performance appraisals, where the default reaction I noticed in myself was to allow all the amazing feedback that I received to be dwarfed by the one or two areas for improvement that were mentioned. Focusing on the negative in this way wastes our time and stalls our progress at all times, but especially in a crisis, so be deliberate about what you allow to influence you.

## I: Implement imperfectly

Once you have enough input to understand what to do next, it's time for the I step in my CRISIS success plan: *Implement imperfectly*. I have to add the imperfectly because so many women, myself included, would rather wait until everything falls into place and we can see the whole staircase before we take the next step. As nice as it would be to have the full perfect picture first time, that almost never happens. Don't allow the 'I'll do it when…' mindset to sneak in here as well. Waiting until everything is perfect and complete is one of the most effective ways to waste time, and potentially miss out on what you are trying to get altogether.

We usually need to take the steps, however imperfect, that we are clear on first, then more clarity inevitably comes with action. I see so many women staying stuck while waiting for all the stars to align, but please don't let that be you. Even if taking imperfect action causes you to make a mistake, you can course correct. I remember reading somewhere once that pilots actually spend a massive amount of flight time course correcting, due to turbulence and other conditions they experience during a flight that can knock a flight off-course. It's the same with you on your journey to having it all. You cannot steer a stationary plane, so I invite you to get moving first, then correct as you go.

One of my incredible clients learnt this powerful truth during the global crisis caused by the Covid-19 pandemic in 2020. She is a mum of two beautiful kids and really wanted to find a job that gave her a sense of fulfilment and purpose but also allowed her the flexibility she needed in order to have time to take care of herself and her family. She had been looking unsuccessfully for over a year, because, in addition to the many challenges faced by women returning to work after having kids, she and her family were also immigrants into the country where they lived, which introduced another major hurdle – a different language being used in the workforce. Then the pandemic hit, causing lockdowns and other restrictions. Her situation felt more and more hopeless, and she was close to giving up when we started working together. I coached her to reignite her vision, her sense of purpose and the 'why' of her goals, which she felt great about, but it was clear that she still felt limited in her ability to find a suitable job due to the lockdowns. Every time it looked as though things might be starting to open up again, there would be another frustrating shut down. Repeatedly, she told me, 'Once they lift the restrictions, then I can take action on what I need to do.' I lovingly challenged her to start implementing imperfectly, with the assumption that the restrictions would never lift. In a little over a month of doing this, she received and accepted an offer for an incredible job. She was absolutely delighted, as this role ticked all the boxes, while also enabling her to use the wealth of experience she had in her professional background.

You too can take your power back from any crisis as you start to implement imperfectly with whatever information and level of freedom you have.

## S: See setbacks as set-ups for success

The final step in the CRISIS success plan is S: *See setbacks as set-ups for success*. In times of crisis and uncertainty there are bound to be setbacks; even more things that you didn't see coming. Please don't give up. Persist and persevere. I know this can be hard, but living a mediocre and unfulfilling life where you don't have all you want is also hard – it's a case of having to choose your hard.

I would rather choose the hard that has reward than the hard that has regret at the end of it.

So many people get to the end of their lives and wish they had taken a chance, that they had done this or that. I don't want that to be me or you, so please persist as setbacks happen. A powerful technique I have found to help me with this is changing my perspective to view setbacks as a set-up for greater success than I was planning and working towards. Looking back at your life thus far, I am sure you can probably think of a few times when you were so disappointed that something you were working towards didn't work out. However, with time and hindsight, you end up being glad it didn't happen the way you wanted because what you got ended up being so much better.

In this step, I invite you to cut out the need for time and hindsight and to just believe that whatever setback you face now is happening *for* you, not *to* you. This will enable you to get back into an empowered and positive frame of mind much more quickly, which is critical to your success. I can't tell you how many times remembering and believing in advance that this simple mantra – this is happening for me, not to me – helped me to quickly pick myself up after being knocked down and get myself back on the road to success – often greater success than I imagined.

I invite you to use these six steps of the CRISIS success plan to stay on course to your destination of 'so much more' and 'having it all' whenever you are hit by a crisis that is out of your control. Giving in to circumstances and allowing them to dictate what you can do or who you can be is not the only option. If you are feeling that way – and trust me, I know that life gives us many opportunities to feel like that – I encourage you to stop, take a few deep breaths, then use the CRISIS plan to take your power back and get back on track to your vision.

Let me end this chapter with one final story about how this plan helped me massively in my own life so you can see how it plays out in an issue so many of us face. One of the many hats I have the privilege of wearing in my business is that of a professional speaker and presenter at events ranging from conferences to company events and award ceremonies. I was invited to host the inaugural Digital Revolution Awards in February 2021, an amazing initiative that was created to celebrate excellence in the Cloud technology industry while raising money for a good cause. The organisers had decided to create the ceremony to reward pioneers in the Cloud industry who had effectively helped keep the world moving forward during the pandemic in 2020. The mass transition made by millions around the world to remote working at that time would simply not have been possible without the hard work of so many in the Cloud industry who provided the necessary technology, so recognising and celebrating their efforts was a big deal. They were also wanting to raise funds through the awards ceremony for St Martin's School, in Kibagare, Kenya, who do a lot of fantastic work helping underprivileged children in Nairobi, so it was important that the event was of a high standard.

Due to pandemic restrictions at the time, the awards ceremony was held virtually. This meant that, as the host, I was responsible for helping to bring the vision and various pre-recorded clips to life in an energetic and engaging manner. My goal was to do an incredible job with this to ensure that the organisers' expectations were exceeded, and also to ensure that plenty of funds were raised for the school in Nairobi. I had so many 'whys' to make this a tremendous success, including believing strongly in the work that organisations like St Martin's do. An organisation like that had helped to lift my father from the abject poverty he grew up in, and through the education they helped make accessible to him, he was able to change the economic trajectory of generations to come.

There were also many 'whys' from a network and business development perspective. There would be so many people watching from top companies around the world; there could be potential collaboration opportunities that emerged. Also, though I had been speaking internationally for several years by this point, I had not really done much hosting like this, so I wanted to do an excellent job of it in the hope that it might lead to many more similar opportunities. I had my vision and my whys, and with those put together, my plan of action for success. Part of that plan involved having plenty of time to prepare in the week leading up to filming, and also ensuring I had plenty of sleep before the event – I had learnt in the past from other speaking commitments that being well rested helps me do a better job and enjoy the experience more.

About ten days before we were scheduled to film, my son, who was around nineteen months old at the time, started having an allergic reaction to almost all his normal food. He would be fine after eating during the daytime, then at about 2am he would wake up and start throwing up violently almost every hour, on the hour, until morning. That in itself was alarming, but in between throwing up he would also suffer explosive diarrhoea that his nappies simply couldn't cope with. It went everywhere – we were changing the sheets several times a night. The hardest part was that my husband and I could see that he was clearly in a lot of pain and distress through it all. It was terrifying, heartbreaking and exhausting to deal with. We got very little sleep, night after night, as my husband and I took it in turns to help our son and deal with all the mess. We went to the doctor and we were told that we should not worry too much, and should expect it to stop soon. It didn't.

Needless to say, I was not preparing for my host role as I would have liked in the week leading up to filming the awards. The night before, I was totally exhausted from all the stress and lack of sleep. I began to panic and wondered what would happen if I totally flopped. It would be terrible for the organisers and for me. I would totally ruin everything for them and never be offered another speaking opportunity.

Thankfully, I know by now to quickly catch myself when running down such unhelpful trains of thought and assured myself that if I could just get a good night's sleep the night before, I could do some accelerated preparation in the taxi on the way to the filming location and it would be fine. I may not have done too much hosting like this in the past, but I am a confident and experienced speaker, which would help. I just needed to be well rested, and it would be fine. So, I went to bed super early that evening, right after putting the kids to bed. The only issue with my plan was that my little boy woke up a little over an hour after I went to bed and proceeded to throw up and poop violently – for literally the entire night.

My husband kept telling me to go to the guest room and rest ahead of the big day, but I couldn't bring myself to leave my precious baby, who was crying nonstop and was clearly in a lot of pain. It was so awful. By the time my alarm went off at 5am, we had just managed to get our son back to sleep but hadn't slept a wink ourselves. I was beyond shattered and officially in crisis mode. Fear gripped me, and I started to panic, wondering how I could ever get through this filming day without letting them down and making a complete fool of myself.

Then I remembered my CRISIS success plan and began to implement it quickly. I started by cutting out the noise – in this case, the negative voices in my head that were telling me that I was screwed, and nowhere near good enough to get through this without looking like a complete idiot. I remembered other times in the past when I had been successful with very little preparation, and I refocused on the vision now, and how much I wanted success for the Cloud talent we were celebrating, for the organisers, for St Martin's School, and for myself. I felt empowered once more after meditating on this for a few minutes.

I then began to inquire intelligently about the best next steps with questions like, 'Where do I need to be today? Should I cancel filming and stay with my boy, or go ahead and do the event?' As I thought about these questions, I heard a clear response of, 'Go, you are meant to film today,' from that familiar inner voice within me. I was clear on where I needed to be, but the usual sense of worry and guilt at having to leave my sick son began to wash over me. It felt worse than ever before due to the physical exhaustion I was dealing with as well, so I continued to inquire intelligently of my intuition.

'What do I need to do to make today a success and overcome tiredness, guilt and worry?'

To my astonishment, the response that came back was, 'Sing'. Sing? I wondered incredulously! Sing what? I definitely didn't feel like singing – especially not after all we'd been through during the night and, quite frankly, over the last ten days. And yet this strange suggestion wouldn't leave, so I figured I might as well try it. Perhaps, on a subconscious level, I knew that singing aloud has tremendous health benefits, which include relieving stress, improving mental health and mood, and enhancing speaking abilities. I went downstairs, far away from the rest of the family, who were still asleep, and went onto YouTube – I figured I was going to need some help from somewhere! I hovered over the YouTube search function, wondering what on earth to sing. In that moment I was reminded of my father-in-law's favourite hymn, 'How Great Thou Art', and how that seemed to lift so much heaviness from us in the church on our wedding day. Singing it made us feel an unbelievable sense of peace despite the terrible grief we were facing.

I was desperate to feel that sense of peace again, so I typed in 'How Great Thou Art', hit search, pressed play on the first lyric video that came up and began to hesitantly sing along. I don't think I have ever felt so ridiculous in all my life. The last thing I wanted to do was sing – scream, cry, go back to try to get some sleep, definitely –, but sing? Absolutely not! Thankfully, I know how powerful that internal wisdom can be, so ignoring my feelings of embarrassment and silliness, I kept singing.

It felt awkward and totally ludicrous for quite a while, but as I continued to sing, I started to feel the stress gradually dissipating, and that familiar sense of peace begin to wash over me. I began to remember that all we had been through this last night and the nights before were just peanuts compared to the possibilities that were available. When the song finished, I hit replay and sang it again, and again. By the time the song was playing for the third time, I had tears of joy streaming down my face and felt like a different woman. I was totally transformed. I had reconnected to that sense of peace that made me feel that, despite the storm, I would be alright. I felt so much better, but I still needed to work out how

I could avoid feeling guilt and worry for leaving my sick son with his dad, who was also due to be working that day. The answer that came to mind was, 'Call your mum.' Thankfully, as we were in the same Covid shielding bubble as my parents, my amazing mum could come over and help my husband in my absence so he could get his work done. She was very happy to be able to help.

Knowing that my son would be in my mother's capable hands helped me to ditch the guilt, but I still felt a bit worried and, quite frankly, exhausted. Days on end of very little to no sleep will do that to you. So I inquired further of my intuition: 'Is there anything else I can do to be successful today?' I was pretty sure I would not be able to break out into song during filming to feel better if I needed to. The response I got was an urge to read something, so I decided to seek input from carefully selected sources – the 'S' in the CRISIS success plan.

I wasn't sure what to read, but as I looked at the phone in my hand I noticed an app full of inspiring writings I'd downloaded a while back; I instinctively clicked it. It opened up to the text for the day function, which randomly selects an inspiring quote or text each day. I clicked on that and saw literally the perfect thing for me to read that morning. It encouraged pausing and meditating in moments of weariness to regain strength for success throughout the day.

The words felt serendipitous, reinforcing what I already knew intuitively, and they were exactly what I needed to read in that moment. I meditated and followed the instructions from the app for a few minutes and felt so supported. That gave me the strength I needed to begin the next step of implementing imperfectly. I got ready, did my hair and make-up, which helped me look and feel more human, and asked for a miracle as I picked up my script and bag and headed out. I then proceeded to fall asleep in the taxi when I should have been preparing. When I woke up, I was so disappointed with myself that I missed the last opportunity to prepare. I was determined to see this setback as a set-up for success, though, so I wiped the drool away from my chin and resolved to give the day my best shot.

I had a few moments during the day when waves of tiredness hit, and I began to fumble lines or felt like giving up. When this happened, I would use it as an opportunity to continue to practise the final step and to see setbacks as a set-up for success. In practical terms, this looked like asking the production crew for a quick break. I would then head to the ladies' toilets to meditate on my vision and re-read the inspiring text from the app that I'd read earlier and practise the suggested meditation and steps until I felt strength for success flood my body once again. Then I'd go back and deliver a performance so many times better than before. The final result was of a much higher standard than many things I had done before, even after a full night's sleep, and it far exceeded the expectations of all involved. The feedback was mind-blowing, and the speaking engagement led to so many more incredible opportunities, including being invited to host both the virtual and glamorous in-person awards ceremony in London year after year.

Looking back over this experience, one of the highlights for me was when my family gathered to watch the inaugural virtual awards ceremony on the day it finally aired. My husband watched it open-mouthed, in total amazement throughout. He couldn't believe how incredible it had turned out, given the mess I was in the morning it was filmed, having had that awful night and the ten days that had preceded it. Hearing him and my daughter say how proud they were of me was the biggest reward ever – I cried more tears of joy. My daughter said she was so inspired by it all, which was so powerful to hear! My baby boy, on the other hand, now thankfully fine health-wise, was utterly unimpressed by the whole thing. We had switched off the cartoon he was watching on TV to watch the awards, and he spent the whole time screaming for the remote to change the channel back. That just goes to show you can't please everyone!

Beyond the pressure of whatever crisis you may be facing are tears of joy after you overcome it. You are powerful enough to overcome anything. I encourage you to believe that, no matter what you are facing, and to use my CRISIS success plan to do just that for you, and your loved ones.

## Key takeaways

- While we may not be able to control what is happening during a crisis, we can always control how we respond to it – and how we respond really does make all the difference.
- How you respond to a crisis can even help turn it, and the chaos it brings with it, into something that can benefit you.
- You can achieve this by implementing the six-step CRISIS success plan to rise above the storm to stay on track.
- The first step in the plan is the C of CRISIS, which stands for **Cut out all the noise** from others, news, etc. This will allow you to access powerful personalised wisdom from within yourself.
- The next step is the two-for-the-price-of-one R that will help you get into the right emotional state in your soul from which

to ask for help, or anything else – an empowered state. You do that by **Remembering past successes** and **Refocusing on your vision**.

- Once you are reconnected to your vision and feeling empowered, it is time for the next step in the CRISIS success plan, I for **Inquire intelligently about your next steps**. You do this by tapping into your intuition.
- The next step is S: **Seek input from carefully selected sources.** After you have inquired about your next steps, it's time to get input and help from others. I can't stress the 'carefully selected sources' part enough.
- Once you have enough input to understand what your best next step should be, it's time for the I step: **Implement imperfectly**.
- The final step in the CRISIS success plan is S: **See setbacks as set-ups for success**. In times of crisis and uncertainty, there are bound to be setbacks, more things that you didn't see coming. Please don't give up. Persist and persevere.
- You can and will succeed if you remember everything is happening *for*, not *to* you.

# Chapter 4: The Curses of Comparison and People-pleasing

How much of your time and life do you waste in the following scenarios:

- Listening to people who mean well but who are actually holding you back from going for new things, and ideas you want to explore.
- Succumbing to the pressure to 'always be on' when working from home, and to staying late when working in the office even when your work is done.
- Struggling to effectively communicate and resolve conflict with other people with challenging personalities, at work, at home or elsewhere.
- Feeling unsure how to navigate obstacles being put in your way, for example, by the queen bee of your department.
- Listening to advice that suggests taking time for self-care, or pursuing your own ambitions is just selfish, and makes you a bad mum.
- Feeling bad about your family and cultural background, which brings with it such high expectations that you never seem to be able to measure up to.

- Navigating life with a partner who is not wholly supportive, so you pretty much have a second full-time job taking care of all the unpaid work, mental load and life admin of running the home.
- Dealing with kids that seem to know how to push all the wrong buttons until they are working on your very last nerve, every single day!

Any of that sound familiar?

I'm almost certain you can add your own examples of how constantly comparing yourself to others, and trying to please them, can totally run your life – but head it in the wrong direction! If you don't relate to others in the right way, a significant amount of your time and life can easily be spent, or rather wasted, going with the flow they set up for you. Life typically gets extremely frustrating and unfulfilling if you settle for spending and wasting your time living up to expectations that others have set for you that have nothing to do with your definition of having it all.

I accidently discovered this dream killer and the strategy to overcome it when I was about twenty-five years old. I was working in the financial services industry in the UK, first at an international bank in Chester as a credit risk analyst, and then as a credit risk consultant for a wonderful boutique consulting firm in the Midlands. While studying, I had rediscovered my love for maths and numbers, and there was plenty of that in my work. I even learnt to write code, which I enjoyed using to help our clients build decision-making scorecards and systems to effectively manage their risk. I was doing well, but after a while I started to get that familiar itch for something more, or at least different. I just wasn't sure what.

For months I suppressed the itch. *Life is good, Maxine, don't rock the boat*, I would think to myself, while trying to forget about it. Except I couldn't. I wondered what was wrong with me. So many of my friends and family would have loved to be in my position, and often told me how lucky I was. I really was lucky: the company was great, so were my colleagues, the money was good, and the job came with all kinds of perks, but when I was alone, away from all the noise and advice, I couldn't shake that feeling that there was something missing.

One weekend, some of the missing pieces came together when I was randomly introduced to a lady by the name of Obi Arinze. She comes from Obosi, the same village in Nigeria as my mum. She has a brilliant mind and was in the process of building an impressive corporate career. When we were introduced, she was a recent Harvard MBA graduate who agreed to pay it forward by having a mentoring conversation with me. I was so blown away and grateful. She asked me about my career, and I explained how things were good, but not necessarily great, and that I wasn't really sure what I wanted to do next.

She suggested that, based on my track record, and what I was feeling now, it was probably a good time to invest in an MBA to learn, broaden my horizons, and figure out my next steps. The thought of an MBA had never seriously crossed my mind before that moment, but as soon as she said it, I knew in my gut it was the right advice for me. She then went on to add that if I was going to do that, she would highly recommend that I apply for a top school like Harvard, because it would open up so many opportunities, as well as the chance to meet incredible people there. I fell silent at her words and my heart sank, as the thought, *people like me don't get into schools like that*, and other such thoughts went through my mind. Before I could politely end the call and return to my life, Obi interrupted, and answered the self-defeating monologue now running through my mind by saying, 'If you're interested in applying, I can mentor you through the process – you definitely have what it takes to get in.'

I couldn't believe it. *What did she say? Wait, she thinks I can get in? She's going to help me? You mean, this is possible?*

I screamed, 'Yes! Please! Thank you!' in quick succession before I could allow those thoughts of self-doubt to come creeping back in to make me mumble excuses and back down. I knew myself well enough to know that I wouldn't want to waste her time and let her down.

Her believing in me and offering to help was exactly what I needed to motivate me, and to keep me on track in order to achieve this unbelievable dream. Over the nine months that followed, she coached me through the detailed and intense application process to get admitted into a world-class MBA programme. The first major hurdle was the GMAT exam, which all applicants need to complete. With her help, I ended up acing it, and scoring in the top 2 per cent of all those who took the exam globally. Then there were the application essays, references and interviews. Through it all, she gave me the support I needed to put in the monumental and stellar effort that finally got me admitted into the Cambridge MBA Class of 2007.

I had the most incredible year studying at the University of Cambridge with brilliant students from forty-five countries around the world and serving as the class Vice President. As a result of these experiences, I was able to launch a fulfilling and successful international career a year later. All this was the 'more' that my soul had been craving when I was working as a consultant in the Midlands.

As a child growing up in Nigeria, the only two international universities I had ever heard of were the prestigious Oxford and Cambridge Universities in the UK. For some reason, I took more of a liking to Cambridge and dreamt that one day it might be nice to go there. After my life took a detour into the catastrophic mess I made of it in my teens, that dream died, and I forgot all about it. It was no longer anywhere near my radar. Even after I got my life back on track and was a successful consultant, prior to meeting Obi, I would never in a million years have believed Cambridge was possible for me.

This simple tweak of not just going with the flow that those around me set up for me, but instead deliberately inviting someone like Obi, who could help me reach my soul's purpose, helped to collapse timelines and catapult me towards my destiny. Mindlessly going with the flow would have killed the unbelievable dream that was trying to come forth. Deliberately inviting the right outside voices like Obi's not only stopped that happening, it also helped resurrect long-forgotten dreams that were always meant to manifest in my life. I kept doing whatever I could to make sure I dealt appropriately with other people who were effectively dream killers my life, and I made a point of inviting the right ones in to influence and catapult me into what seemed impossible. I have since discovered that this strategy can be one of the most effective for those of us seeking to keep on track to find our purpose, reach our goals, and have it all. I have therefore continued to use this strategy; I coach clients to do the same and they achieve incredible timeline-collapsing success in their lives and families.

## Overcoming this dream killer

There is a better way to live so that other people don't run, and ultimately ruin, your life. Rather than mindlessly spending and wasting time, comparing yourself to others and living under the weight of others' expectations, I invite you to invest a little bit of time in implementing the simple strategy I stumbled upon during my destiny-defining experience with Obi. It helped me stop settling for a good job, as some people were pressuring me to, when in fact I was destined for far more by pursuing my MBA at Cambridge and beyond. The time investment of just a few thirty-minute conversations with her over the course of nine months changed my entire life and career for the better. You too can experience results that will change your entire life trajectory as you begin to invest some of your time to implement this strategy.

I like to think of the strategy as deliberately designing a personal board of directors that is conducive to helping you reach your vision. I use the words 'deliberately designing' here because when we are not intentionally designing our personal board, guess who is on the board by default? As you might have guessed, it's other people – people who may mean well, but whose advice may lead you to waste time taking your life in a direction that is not aligned with your definition of having it all. You definitely don't want them running the show in your life. I therefore invite you to invest time to first dismantle the default personal board of directors full of 'the others', and in its place deliberately design a board that is supportive of your vision. Doing this has been so powerful for me and my coaching clients, and I am sure it will be for you too, collapsing the timeline for reaching your vision of having it all and empowering you to get rid of so much of the guilt that we can sometimes deal with. This strategy will also be incredibly effective at making your impossible-looking goals possible, because it can fast-track you towards your vision of so much more for you, your family and your life.

Before we continue into more details on exactly how to implement this strategy, it's worth quickly defining what I mean by your personal board of directors. If you think of a board of directors in the traditional business sense, its key purpose is to ensure the company's wellbeing and prosperity by collectively directing its affairs while meeting the appropriate interests of its shareholders and stakeholders. In the context of your life, your personal board of directors should ideally ensure your wellbeing and prosperity by helping you direct your affairs so you navigate and overcome your unique challenges and thrive in, rather than just survive in, work and life. At the same time, they should ensure that you meet the appropriate interests of important loved ones such as your children, your partner – if you have one – your boss, your colleagues, your wider family and friends, and so on.

Your board should include anyone and anything that could have that kind of positive influence on you, and should exclude anyone and anything whose influence has the opposite effect. The issue that so many women face is that we haven't invested the time to deliberately design and then go on to build our personal board of directors to influence us. Instead, we are constantly influenced and living under the weight of the expectations of a default personal board of directors – people and things that just happen to be there. The awful thing is that their actions and impact on us is often guilt-inducing, in opposition to our vision and purpose, and far from conducive to our holistic wellbeing and prosperity. Maybe it's the expectations in society and in your culture that dictate what a 'good mum' should do, that you can never seem to measure up to, or what your own mother and other female family members have set as a standard – a standard that is so exhausting and unattainable for you to even try to meet. Perhaps it's the friends that seem to have it all together compared to you, along with the social media channels that keep you posted on all said friends' activities. Every day that you log on to Facebook, there's another reason to feel crap about yourself and how well everyone is doing compared to you. Maybe it's the partner who doesn't do anywhere near the same amount of unpaid work around the house that you do, leaving you feeling exhausted, resentful and unable to stop the to-do list that is running riot in your mind, or the absence of anyone on your default board who has been where you want to go, and is able to challenge, stretch and help you like Obi did for me. It could even be all the above!

The good news is that it doesn't have to be this way. One of the greatest gifts you can give yourself is to dismantle the default board that wastes your precious time and may be keeping you on a never-ending Mama guilt trip, and deliberately design one that will support and even catapult you towards your dream destination of having it all. I like to call this process 'Activating Your Personal Board of Directors', and you can do this in three simple steps:

1. Uncover the challenges
2. Fire negative board members
3. Hire positive board members

## Step 1: Uncover the challenges

Let's start with uncover the challenges. This step is all about determining the biggest challenges that you are currently facing, specifically around creating your vision of 'so much more', in which you are achieving your own goals while also taking amazing care of yourself, your family and your running to-do list. Basically, your definition of having it all.

You uncover the challenges by looking at your vision and asking yourself honestly, *What could hold me back from achieving this vision?*

Could it be the fact that you don't feel confident enough to be able to pull it off? Perhaps you have no clue where to even begin? Or perhaps you don't know how to bring up with your boss and other colleagues the fact that you need a bit more flexibility in your daily life due to commitments to your kids? Or maybe it's that you don't have any time for yourself to even think about self-care, never mind practise it. Perhaps it's that you continually find yourself shouting at the kids and family you deeply love out of frustration, then you feel so terrible for doing that.

Whatever it is for you, take a moment, think about it, then write down as many of these challenges as you can come up with. There is something so powerful and freeing about getting everything out of your head and onto paper or any other note-taking device, so, please, gift yourself that experience and take a few moments to do that now.

When you have all that down, select your top three challenges in your personal life and in your professional life to create a total of six challenges that are hindering your ability to make your vision a reality. Make the list relevant for you – if, for example, there is some overlap of a challenge that impacts both work and life, make a list of five, or if you are not working at the moment, keep it to a list of five or six personal life challenges. Once you have your list, you've completed step one.

## Step 2: Fire negative board members

You're now ready to move to the second step, which is to fire any negative board members. What I mean by this is you want to limit how much you are influenced by the people or things that make these personal and professional challenges more difficult. Think of yourself on your journey to your vision of 'having it all'. Then reflect on questions like, *what people or things make me feel like it will be impossible to reach my destination?* or, *what people or things make me feel guilty, bad about myself, or wrong for wanting what I want?*

Anything or anyone that contributes in a negative way to the challenges you uncovered is on the list to be fired, but it's important to mention a couple of considerations here. The people on this list may not necessarily be bad people – they may be well-meaning and have good intentions, and I'm definitely not suggesting that you call them up and tell them they are fired, nor am I suggesting that you cut them out of your life altogether. The important thing here is that these individuals may not understand the vision in your head, and while they might be trying to help, they could also be hindering your progress by advising you against making the necessary steps towards achieving your goals.

I myself experienced this when I spoke to friends who thought I was mad for wanting something more when I supposedly had it made with my consulting job. I fired these default board members who made me feel bad about this; I simply didn't waste my time talking to them about my career anymore. We were still friends who talked about other things going on in our lives, but I stopped allowing their opinions on my career to influence my plans and how I was feeling about them.

It is so important to be selective with what information you share with certain people because, sadly, not everyone will understand and be supportive. Everyone is on their own journey through life, with their own challenges, worries, hopes, perspectives, opinions, past hurts and experiences. Whatever they do or say to you is very likely going to be filtered through the lens of all that and more. Depending on the maze through which their advice is coming, many well-meaning people may end up doing or saying something that keeps you away from your true vision and purpose. If, for example, you are trying to do something that no one in your family has ever done before as part of your huge vision, your well-intended mum or other relative may advise you not to get your hopes up, in an attempt to protect you from the hurt they experienced when their own dreams were stifled. This in turn starts making you doubt your own ability to succeed.

I saw this play out with one of my clients. She was struggling with feeling like she would never have a sense of balance between her work and life. I introduced her to this concept of activating her personal board of directors. When she uncovered her biggest challenges and reviewed her default board, she realised that she had two major board members who were negatively impacting her. The first was her sister, who was really struggling with everything as she tried to balance her own career and family life with two kids. Her sister was not focused on trying to improve her situation at that moment, and kept telling my client things like, 'Just watch, you're going to have exactly the same problems when your kids get to this age, your life will be a total nightmare.' My client began to waste time worrying about these predictions, and over the years she actually began to step into each nightmare her sister predicted – more time wasted, as you can imagine. My client also spent quite a bit of time looking at everyone's perfect highlights on social media and comparing these to her own life, which made her feel worse about her challenges. When she identified these negative board members that made her challenges worse, she fired them by basically reducing the level of influence they had on her – and it was powerful!

With her sister, she 'fired' her by making herself less available for the conversations that were all doom and gloom about motherhood, and she found that gradually the predictions of all the problems she would supposedly face stopped happening as frequently. When she faced the genuine issues that come up for us as parents, during our sessions she was able to get coaching support to overcome them. When it came to social media, she unfollowed a couple of people and halved the time she spent on it, which, in her own words, made a world of difference. We all have these influences in our lives that go completely against what it is that we actually want, but we have unconsciously let them be there, wasting our time and making us feel worse.

To create and achieve what we want, we need to reduce these negative influences in our lives. It can be tough to implement this, especially when there are people like family involved, but it is so worth building the people and communication skills to do this effectively and assertively to ensure that these people will truly respect your choices. Such people and situations are typically drains on your time and energy, and it's therefore so important to tackle them head on. Once you fire them from having such an influence on you, you tend to have much more time and energy to be able to create and activate the supportive board that can step up and really help you in your situation.

## Step 3: Hire positive board members

This all leads us nicely into step three of activating your personal board of directors, which is to hire positive board members. These are the people and things that, when you are around them, empower you to overcome the challenges you uncovered and move you closer to your dream destination that you envisioned, just as Obi did for me. Look through your own personal list of challenges and consider questions like:

*Who or what could I 'hire' to help me move closer to my vision?*

*What influences could I introduce into my life to help solve or ease the challenges I uncovered?*

When you get an idea, if it involves someone else, reach out to them immediately to start the process. I've found that there is no better time than right now to take steps towards your dreams. Tomorrow often never comes, because the 'I'll do it when...' mindset can sneak in and rob us of momentum when we put things off. So, if you need to literally pause reading for a while to contact someone so that it's done, please go for it.

Let me give you a couple of examples of what hiring positive board members might look like, to give you an idea of who or what could be a great personal board member to hire. I work with a lot of ambitious women who want to progress in their careers but find themselves with the challenge of no female role models to inspire and guide them, especially through the challenge of how to achieve their career goals without having to sacrifice their health and family life. This all has an impact on their confidence to succeed in high stakes and high visibility roles.

This is the exact challenge that was being faced by one of my clients, a brilliant mum of two kids. She also felt that, due to overt and unconscious bias in the organisation she was working for, it was pretty much impossible for a woman, never mind for a woman of colour like herself, to reach the top, as she aspired to do. When I suggested that she 'hire' someone already at the top of the organisation to her personal board of directors as a mentor, I sensed her hesitation and knew intuitively it was because no one at the top looked anything like her.

I encouraged her to reach out anyway, because in my experience, regardless of physical appearance, all potential board members look like you if you are ready to see that. Remember, everything you see, including you and me, is made up of atoms, which are mostly invisible. As nice as it would be to find someone whose less than one per cent looks like ours, it's not always possible, especially when we are dreaming big like my client was, and as I hope you are. Regardless of gender or race, we are all part of the human race; under our skin, we have the same organs, and we all bleed red. We are all more alike than we are different. I shared that with her, and added the fact that sometimes you can't find role models who physically look like you, because *you* are who you are looking for! You are the first one, especially in this rapidly changing world.

In times like this, you have to find the courage to do what it takes to be the first; to be the person who can pave the way as a role model for other women. Ancient wisdom advises us that if you seek, you will find. That works equally well for career-limiting ceilings, as well as for people who will have the effect of helping you grow wings to fly over those ceilings and thus make them irrelevant to you. If you choose to focus on your limitations, you will always have limitations to focus on.

I shared these reasonings with my client and advised her to be brave and ask one of the top leaders to mentor her. I concluded with, 'The worst answer you will get is no, and last time I checked, no to a request like this never killed anyone.' She hesitantly agreed to approach an older white gentleman to mentor her on what it would take to become a top leader in the company. He was very glad to help. Within eighteen months of using his advice on the professional front, and my advice for other things, she broke all performance records within her role, adding hundreds of millions of dollars to their bottom line. She was then promoted to become the leader of one of the company's most important and fastest-growing regions. She is the first woman of colour to ever achieve such results and such a promotion in the company's long history. This impressive feat would have remained impossible if she had not hired the right board member to take her natural brilliance to the next level and get her to where she wanted to go.

Please don't waste too much time looking or waiting to hire personal board members whose less than one per cent looks like yours – the truth is, they may not exist, as was the case for my client.

The world has changed so much over a short period of time, and much remains uncertain, so even if you do find a female role model, your path to a similar position may well look very different to hers. So it's advisable to 'hire' as many allies as possible, in addition to female role models, to your board as well. During one of hundreds of research interviews I had with professional women while writing this book, one incredibly accomplished female leader mentioned how regular chats with her male allies helped her get over her tendency to be quiet and to second-guess herself in meetings, even though she had something to say. Following their advice to regularly pitch in, even with far-from-perfect ideas, has had a profound and positive impact on her career.

Another major challenge I see many women facing is the struggle of having to do most of the unpaid work at home. In so many cases, although both my clients and their partners do paid work outside the home, the housework split is nowhere near 50/50, so one party grudgingly does most of it. As we explore their specific issues during our coaching sessions, in many cases, it becomes apparent that my clients have never clearly shared with their partners the expectations that they would each be responsible for half the housework, or spelled out what that needed to look like. As one woman said, 'I feel he should know, especially as we have a young son that I am solely responsible for breastfeeding.'

While I totally agree that it would be great and right for him and other partners to just know intuitively what needs to be done by them, sadly he didn't, and it seems that tends to be so in many instances. In this case, her husband grew up in a home where his mother was a stay-at-home mum who did everything, so he left my client to get on with it, because no one had told him otherwise, and so she just kept doing it all, albeit resentfully most of time. We explored potential solutions, as I do with all clients, and we looked at what made sense for their home and relationship. The result was an honest conversation about how she was feeling, her expectations of a 50/50 unpaid work split, as well as introducing a visual housework roster, the new board member she chose to hire, on their already-existing family calendar. They worked together to split things fairly – like taking out the bins, cooking and washing up – then scheduled it all on the roster. When one of them had a busy paid-work week on the calendar, the other compensated by doing more of the home stuff, but otherwise it was split equally. So far, it's working brilliantly. The only small hiccup I've seen occur is that my clients often joke that their partners don't do some of the housework as well as they would have, but they can live with that, as things are so much less stressful now. I am always so happy to hear this, as we definitely all need fewer stressors in life as women and as mothers, as well as more true partnership.

Please don't allow the default board members of others' expectations and societal norms to keep you stuck in an outdated lifestyle that does not work for who you are and, more importantly, for who you aspire to be. The solutions I mentioned above may not be the right ones for you, but finding what will work for you is straightforward. It is a fantastic investment of time to take a few minutes for yourself to tap into your powerful internal wisdom by asking yourself some questions that will help you uncover what will work for you and your family.

Even if you are currently a stay-at-home mum whose partner is the sole breadwinner, it is quite possible that the unpaid work at home is more than the paid work happening outside the home, so your partner can help at home as well. Ideally, you want to get to some sort of equal split of the total of unpaid and paid work done by you both. You deserve true partnership not just for yourself so that you can have free time to relax, read a book or do whatever you want to do, but also because of the impact you will be having on the next generation as you create a true and fair partnership for yourself. Remember social learning theory? Our kids are watching and learning, and modelling equality at home is an even greater result, to me, of this agreement than the additional free time you achieve for yourself.

This need for true and fair partnership really is so much bigger than any of us and our individual homes. A big through-line in my work since I started my business has been helping to empower and elevate women so that we can make progress in the fight for gender equality. Right now, according to statistics, it could be well over one hundred years before we see equal pay for men and women, which is totally unacceptable to me. I have worked with individuals and companies on this over the years, listening and suggesting strategies, and one thing is crystal clear to me from my experience: we can win a large part of this battle for equality at home. It is healthy and necessary for our sons and daughters to see the unpaid work done by their parents at home being shared fairly. As nice as it would be for our partners to just know that they should split the housework evenly, sadly a huge number don't.

Again, because of how the world has changed compared to the one that your partner may have grown up in, the division of labour between their parents that they observed in their home may not work for you and the life and family you are trying to create now. Those often unspoken expectations are negative board members that need to be confronted and fired. If you find yourself in this situation, I invite you to do three things:

1. Tap into your internal wisdom to get clear on what you want from your partner so that the partnership is fair in your opinion.
2. Confidently ask for it so that they are made aware of your expectations.
3. Work together to create it.

If needed, hire an appropriate personal board member to get some coaching or support to do this effectively, both for yourself and for the next generation that is relying on you to model this important example of equality. With this and all your other challenges, hopefully you can see how crucial it is to carefully curate who is influencing and advising you. If you have a friend who already has an amazing partnership with her husband, she might be a great board member to 'hire' to hear more about how she got there. It would also be a good idea to 'fire' those friends who just want to complain about their partners without focusing on potential solutions to the issue.

If you're busy at work, challenged for time and not a fan of cooking, you may want to fire the friend who makes you feel like a bad mum because you're not baking bread and making gourmet meals for your family every night and instead get hold of the latest 'meals in minutes' cookbook. If you feel that starting a profitable business could be your way of avoiding the motherhood penalty, you may want to fire the well-meaning family and friends who try to protect you by telling you that starting a business is risky and hard.

Some great board members you may want to hire include a business coach, a businesswomen's network, or even time with a great book, sharing successful start-up stories and strategies. If you are lacking confidence and a strategy to achieve a goal or overcome a challenge, look to hire a mentor or coach who has been there, who will guide you and save you time as you learn from their mistakes.

For those who have found themselves shouting at their family out of frustration and then feeling bad about it, like I have, it may be worth enlisting the support of parenting and relationship coaches. I did this, and it worked beautifully! The key is to get to know yourself and what you want, then to hire and fire board members accordingly – you can't just leave it to chance.

Another quick tool I like to use to help me decide on who to hire or fire from my personal board of directors is my dream destination versus guilt-trip check. I assess all the people and things that currently influence me and ask myself, do they help me move towards my dream destination of having it all, or do they make me feel Mama guilt? If it's the latter, I fire them by not giving them a place of influence in my life; if it's the former, I hire them. With anyone I hire, I also ensure that, from time to time, I include people quite far ahead of me, such as Obi, to expedite the journey towards my vision and highest potential.

In order to make the most of the opportunity during time spent with mentors and others that I hire to help me in any way, as well as to ensure that I'm being respectful of their time, I always invest time prior to meeting with them to tap into my internal wisdom to prepare. I ask myself questions like:

**How can I make the most of this opportunity with this individual?**

**What do I want to learn from them, given what they have been through?**

**How can I also add value back to them to create a win-win situation, if possible?**

Having a deliberately designed personal board of directors will also help with getting your to-do list more under control, as you'll be doing more of the things that move you closer to your vision and fewer of the things that don't. So, go ahead and schedule some time right now to complete the exercises above and get clear on who or what you need to hire and fire from your personal board of directors, and what you need to do to move closer to true partnership at home. Then commit to get to work on it – for you and your precious family. You'll be so glad you did.

Let me end with this quick story of how I personally did this and got started on my journey to true partnership with my husband Nnamdi. When I got married, I moved to be with my husband, then had my daughter, but I didn't really have a vision – I was just happy to be starting a new life with my love. The default board of directors I had around me were amazing women who were great wives and mums; they cooked, they cleaned, they baked, they literally did all the domestic things!

Coming from Nigerian culture, the standard is high for these duties, so I got to work trying to keep up, in spite of the fact that I have never been able to stand most of this sort of work and I was battling postnatal depression – something I only realised with hindsight. I was exhausted and miserable a lot of the time – each day seemed like an endless treadmill of work and chores, with no end in sight. One day, in the middle of trying to do it all, I snapped and burst into tears in the kitchen. I just couldn't take it anymore!

My husband came running in from the football game he was watching and asked what was wrong. I went into a long screaming rant about how sick I was of it all, the endless laundry, cooking, cleaning and everything. Once I got it all out, it felt so good to have finally let him see how frustrated I was with him not helping and leaving me to carry so much on my own. I wiped my runny nose with my sleeve and looked defiantly at him for his response, ready for an argument if he dared say or even look like he was thinking the wrong thing. I was so stunned when he simply said, 'Who asked you to do all that?'

'Huh?' was the only response I could get out, through my shock.

'I'm happy to help,' he continued, 'I mean, I was doing it all before you moved here, but as you started doing it all, I left you to it.'

Wow! It had never occurred to me to plan how we would get stuff done, or to let him into the conversations in my head about all the expectations I had that he wasn't living up to. I had created a living nightmare for myself, and probably for him too, with my regular passive-aggressive comments made in frustration prior to this big meltdown. I made the decision there and then to fire other people's standards and definitions of being a good wife and mother from my personal board of directors. I came up with my own vision, which included a 50/50 partnership with my husband, and we began to create it. As we are a dual-career couple, we literally hired help for some the housework. Whenever hiring help was impossible, we made sure the unpaid work was split fairly. I cooked meals, he cleaned up and did the dishes. I did the laundry, he did the ironing, and so on, all while our kids watched and viewed this as normal, which it is for us now, and for the world that I hope our kids will go on to live in. My hope is that this instils in them the belief that they can be whatever they want to be in life, without being limited by gender and culture stereotypes, or anything else. My family is far from perfect, and we are still a work in progress, but it's working so much better than the default way that we were living before. I feel fulfilment and gratitude, rather than frustration and resentment, when I think of what I get to do at home for my loved ones, and the work I am blessed to do in the world.

My set-up may not be your perfect set-up, but you owe it to yourself and your loved ones to ditch the suggestions from your dream-killing default board full of 'the others' and discover what works for you, so you can fire and hire the right board members to help you create and start living your dream life.

## Key takeaways

- You don't have to go with the flow that 'the others' around you suggest for you.
- Investing time to activate your personal board of directors by dismantling the default board that just happens to be there, and deliberately designing one that supports your dream and vision is one of the most impactful things you can do for your time and life.
- Activate your personal board of directors by uncovering the challenges stopping you from creating your vision of 'having it all', then firing negative board members and hiring positive ones.

- Use the dream destination versus guilt-trip check to help decide who or what to hire and fire. Assess all the people and things that do or could influence you and ask yourself if they help you move towards your dream destination of having it all. Or do they make you feel Mama guilt? If it's the latter, fire them by not giving them a place of influence in your life; if it's the former, hire them.

- If you have a partner, it is important to create a true partnership where the unpaid work at home is fairly split, if you don't already have this. You deserve true partnership, not just for yourself but for the next generation who are watching and learning from you.

# Chapter 5: Not Putting on Your Own Oxygen Mask First

If you often feel like you have to put yourself last, because you are constantly busy and have to wait for the moment when you can find time after taking care of everyone, or working through your to-do list before you can take time for yourself, it's likely you are being robbed of time, purpose and your dream of having it all by not putting on your own oxygen mask first. So many mums, myself included in the past, are being robbed blind by this one. It leads us to make up these rules that dictate that we can't relax or take care of whatever it is that we want for ourselves until this or that gets done first.

As anyone who has ever listened to the safety briefing on a flight knows, if we took that approach in the event of an emergency onboard, everyone, including the loved ones we are trying to help, would very likely suffer. It's exactly the same here on the ground, emergency or not.

My time studying for my MBA at Cambridge was so incredible, and conducive to the career acceleration I had been craving. Post-graduation, I was launched into a successful international career in which I was recognised as one of the top thirty individuals under the age of forty in my industry. I took on a variety of leadership roles in organisations with high performance cultures that developed my skills and provided plenty of challenging opportunities to leverage them for success. For a few years, regardless of the role, country or culture that my work immersed me in, I was able to put in the work to replicate, and often exceed, past successes. It was extremely hard work doing all this, but I was happy to, because the career success gave me a sense of worth. Against all odds, I had made something out of my life, and people loved the results. I would burn the candle at both ends to keep it up and impress whoever it was that needed to be impressed, or to exceed whatever the current quarterly business target was. Feelings of exhaustion would pop up from time to time, but I would suppress them, because I liked being busy. I started to treat being busy as a sort of badge of honour that made me feel important and needed; like some kind of superwoman that manages to do and succeed at everything.

I loved answering the question 'How are you?' with something along the lines of, 'Oh, I am so busy, flying to New York next week to do this, that and the other, for work and everyone else,' before pausing to secretly enjoy the usual admiring looks and comparisons to superwoman that followed. Internally, I was also telling myself that I had no other choice but to work so hard. I needed to ensure that I was exceeding what was required of me at work, as my bosses had high expectations from Cambridge grads. Plus, I needed to do whatever I could to make my parents proud, and to keep making things up to them – I had put them through so much. Then there were the loans! I still needed to pay off the tens of thousands of pounds' worth of student loans

I'd taken out for my studies. All these things, and so much else that I needed to do for others, left little space to even think about what I needed to do for me.

I continued on with my hamster wheel of frenzied self-sacrificial activity until one day, totally unexpectedly, I was completely burnt out and ended up being hospitalised with stress. After refusing to listen to my body's continual requests for rest, it eventually forced me to take it. I was in pain and bedridden for weeks, unable to do even the smallest things for myself. This was terrifying, and extremely humbling for the independent superwoman persona I was trying, and now failing, to project. I wanted to look like I had it all together, and the last thing I wanted to do was to ask anyone for help, as I believed that was a sign of weakness. During this time, however, I was forced to ask for help, as I literally could not help myself. The most eye-opening thing about this awful experience was that the very people I thought I was helping by sacrificing what I wanted and needed were the ones that were most inconvenienced by my breakdown. I had to move back home at thirty for my parents to look after me, and my work suffered tremendously – I was barely able to achieve ten per cent of what was expected of me. To say I was embarrassed of myself and what my life had become would be putting things mildly. This led me to a very dark place mentally where I did everything to avoid anyone and anything that I didn't absolutely have to deal with. The last thing I wanted to do was answer the inevitable 'How are you?' question. What would I say if I couldn't answer with 'busy'?

I regularly questioned the point of my existence. *Who am I if I'm not achieving anything impressive and I'm failing everywhere?* I wondered. *What am I worth if I have nothing to show for my day? How can I just be lying here? I need to be doing something!* Except, I physically couldn't. I was forced by my body to lie there and wrestle with these and similar thoughts and questions for weeks. The blow of this excruciating process was softened by my family, who showed me unconditional love that didn't require me to do a single thing in return. As they poured into me selflessly, I started to see that my worth and value was not tied to anything that I had to do or achieve, but to who I am. As I regularly tried to apologise for inconveniencing them, I was repeatedly hushed and told, 'The body needs rest! Enjoy the rest you need and deserve.' Over time, I started to see how deceived I was when I was trying to be a superwoman. I had been telling myself that I would rest when I completed the next milestone, goal or event, except it never came. I am ambitious, so there was always something else to do that kept me running on my hamster wheel, existing on fumes, until I finally crashed and burnt out. After weeks of soul searching on that bed, things finally seemed so clear.

Obviously, a body needs rest, and if you don't willingly give it, it will have to take it by force. I didn't need to do anything to deserve rest; it was my body's right, and totally necessary for the benefit of me and everyone around me! In that moment, I vowed to make changes in my life when I got better, and that's exactly what I did. I had no idea how to do this, so I decided to hire my first ever life and career coach onto my personal board of directors. She had achieved the level of success I wanted to reach in her career, and also seemed to have an incredible marriage and family life that inspired me greatly as a then single woman who wanted that too. I invested several thousands of pounds into her programmes, and even flew out to her international seminars to learn her secrets. It was worth every single penny and second of time invested. Within a few months of learning from her, and implementing the coaching, I was more successful than I had ever been at work, with less effort than I had ever put in. I went from barely achieving ten per cent of what was expected to well over two hundred per cent, all while having plenty of time for rest and self-care.

I learnt how to incorporate time for me and what I needed and wanted first into my schedule, and then, through that, to give work the best version of me that naturally overachieves without stress. It was almost unbelievable. Perhaps the most incredible aspect of this whole turnaround was what happened when I started making room for my personal desires. I received an invitation from one of my cousins, Chuks, to travel from London to Stavanger, in Norway, to become his son David's godmother during his baptism. I doubt the old 'busy superwoman' version of me would have managed to find the time to go, even though she would no doubt have been as excited to be asked as the new version of me was. I reorganised my calendar as I had learnt to, in order to make space for what I really wanted to do for me. I made my bookings, excitedly counted down the days, and finally boarded the flight that weekend in January 2012, not realising that trip would change my life forever. It was incredible to see my cousin and his beautiful family again, and to meet so many of their friends from Norway and elsewhere who had gathered for the event. One of them was a handsome guy by the name of Nnamdi, who had been classmates with Chuk's wife Chisom at Imperial College London, where they had studied petroleum geoscience a few years prior. He was now also living in Norway and had remained such close friends with the family that they had asked him to be David's godfather.

Nnamdi and I immediately hit it off at our mutual godson's baptism. We communicated nonstop after the event and arranged trips back and forth between Norway and the UK to see each other. Things went so amazingly well that we were engaged by December that same year. We got married the following May, after which I moved to Norway.

It was like my wildest dreams were coming true, and the icing on the cake was when we welcomed our precious daughter Chiamaka into the world in July 2015. I wish I could say that when I became a mum I remembered my hard-earned lesson of needing to put on my own oxygen mask first, but unfortunately, I didn't. As is the case with so many other mums, my own needs fell lower and lower down the priority list. From the outside looking in, I was finally living the dream; I had the career, the man, the house and the baby that I'd always wanted. On the inside, however, the dream felt more like a nightmare at times. I often found myself totally overwhelmed and miserable. No one had prepared me for how hard those things would be that I had assumed were basic aspects of motherhood. Let's start with the perfect example: breastfeeding!

I am not sure where I learnt this, but I got the idea that breast-feeding would be a perfect and idyllic bonding opportunity for me and my child that would have me smiling and looking down lovingly at her as she fed every three hours. Imagine then the shock I experienced when the sheer pain of it made me want to scream, and resulted in me spending most of my day trying to keep clothes from touching my chest due to the constant pain. Add to that the post-natal hormones that quite frankly had me wondering how I would ever be able to get through those early days with just me and the baby and no adult conversation without totally losing my mind. Then there were the endless things to do – the cooking, cleaning, stuff around the house.

When you're originally from Nigeria like I am, there's a huge amount of pressure to be the good Nigerian wife and mum that takes things to a whole new level through her innate ability to take care of everything and everyone seamlessly. Never one to turn down a challenge, I did my best to live up to the role, all the while being sleep deprived due to my new baby's schedule. Unsurprisingly, I was exhausted – physically, emotionally and mentally. I was so busy trying to look after everyone and everything else that I didn't have a moment to myself, and even if I had, I wouldn't have known what to do with it.

Constantly putting myself last caused me to lose all sense of who I was, and what I even wanted. I felt like I was back on my little hamster wheel once again, going through the motions and not really sure how to make it all stop. I knew I was blessed to be in Norway, where we had up to one year of paid maternity leave, and while I wished, and still do, that every woman around the world had the same opportunity and choice, I honestly wondered how in the world I was going to make it through that year. I felt like one big emotional mess most of the time, and each look through my Facebook feed confirmed it to me: yep, you're definitely one hot mess. While my friends were posting amazing photos and videos, I could barely remember what day of the week it was, as I struggled unsuccessfully to get my house clean. One day, I had the clever thought that perhaps I would feel better if I joined some of the mum support groups I found online – BIG mistake. Rather than make me feel better, reading all the posts made me feel doomed. It was as though each rant, each meltdown, each joke about all the stress of motherhood driving mums to want to down a whole bottle of wine that I read in those groups made me realise, oh my goodness, this is it! When you have kids, forget about you and what you want – it's all about them. I would read their well-intended quotes like, 'Once you bring kids into the world, it's not about you anymore,' and, 'No matter what happens, kids come first,' or the dreaded, 'You have to sacrifice everything to be a good mother,' and I would totally freak out that I must be a bad mother for not doing all these things naturally and gladly.

The guilt was unbearable, so I tried my best to be a good mother, putting Chiamaka first and sacrificing, until one night I couldn't take it anymore. I'd just done the late-night feed, then I put my daughter to bed, went into the bathroom and bawled my eyes out, partly from the stinging pain in my nipples, but mostly from the stinging pain in my heart. I couldn't even recognise the woman looking back at me in the streaky mirror. I looked a mess, felt a mess and was a mess! I wondered, *How can this be my life? This is definitely not what I envisioned growing up.* Mentally, it felt like I was back in that room in Soho surrounded by crushing circumstances and wondering, as that pimp had asked me, 'What choice do you have anyway?' *Isn't this what good mothers have to do? They put everyone else first and sacrifice. All the other mums seem to be coping fine – what's wrong with you? There must be something wrong with me*, I thought. *I'm not good enough.* At this point, I was sobbing loudly and couldn't care less if my husband woke up.

Actually, I secretly hoped he would, because it would be nice for him to understand just how hard things had been for me. It seemed as though his life had just gone on as normal after the birth of our daughter, while mine had totally fallen apart. I sat on the grey tiles on the bathroom floor, back against the door, sobbing and wondering how my life had come to this, and whether there was any way for me to feel happy and fulfilled as a 'good mum'. Just then, I heard a familiar voice within me say, 'This is not who you are meant to be, you are meant for so much more!'

I sat upright as a chill went down my spine on hearing those familiar words of wisdom. It had been a while since I had tapped into this wisdom, and it clearly showed in how I was feeling and living. My mind went back once again to that night in Soho, to the first time I heard those words that radically changed, and ultimately saved, my life. From the outside looking in, I was in a totally different set of circumstances as I sat there on my heated bathroom floor, compared to that freezing night all those years ago. On the inside, though, the mental prison felt exactly the same. I felt stuck, and like I had no choice but to do what my circumstances suggested, even though I really didn't want to go where they were leading me.

As I pondered those words again, I slowly began to come back to my senses. My life experience had showed me over and over again that anything is possible; that I didn't have to settle for what circumstances suggest; that I was meant for more, even if I couldn't see how yet. I had also learnt that how alive and aligned with my purpose I felt on the inside was way more important than what my life looked like on the outside. I felt more successful standing on that freezing Soho street after making a firm decision to change than I did sitting here in my warm, lovely home, despite the fact that I had nothing back then but three pound coins and a mind full of purpose and possibility. I felt a million times better with just that than I did in this perfect-looking life I was trying, and desperately failing, to create. Something had to change, but what, I inquired, listening intently, and how?

'Just like before, shut out all the noise, tap into your powerful internal guidance, and what looks and feels impossible will become your reality, exactly like before.'

That was all I needed to hear. Right there and then, I made another firm decision, to make it non-negotiable to consistently check in with my internal wisdom; to use it to get guidance about how to put on my mask first, to take care of me first, then others. Taking care of myself is so much more than just looking after my physical body through rest and other things, like the massage I wanted so badly but had been putting off until that moment when I had time. It is about looking after all of me – my physical body, as well as my emotional and mental health, and so much more. Guided by my internal wisdom, I started making both small and significant shifts to look after all of me, and it gradually transformed my life beyond recognition.

One of them was to get enrolled in a part-time coaching certification programme during my maternity leave to help with my mental health. I received this idea when I asked two great questions of my intuition. First, 'How can I add enriching and meaningful adult conversation to my days as a new mum?' And second, 'What can I do to satisfy this ambitious, goal-driven side of myself that seems to have got lost since I became a mum?' There is no way I could have dreamed then that investing a few minutes to get that guidance, then a bit more time over the course of my maternity leave to complete that certification would lead to this: thousands of lives being positively impacted by the business I would go on to start, and ultimately leading me to write this book, which I hope radically transforms your life beyond recognition too. I used to think that putting on my own oxygen mask first was selfish, but these life experiences helped me see that it is actually one of the most selfless things you can do as a mum. Not putting on your own oxygen mask first eventually robs you, and those around you, of so much time, quality of life and purpose. So many people's breakthroughs are on the other side of you saying yes to you first – don't allow this to get robbed from you, and them.

## Overcoming this dream killer

Having been through those awful experiences, I find the thought of being the busy superwoman that women in many cultures around the world admire, and aspire to be, so boring and uninspiring. It is definitely not my definition of 'having it all'. This is not meant to judge or criticise anyone who lives or wants to live that way; as I said before, I've been there, and each mum gets to define 'having it all' in her own way. For me, though, the constantly busy super-woman lifestyle is utterly unsustainable due to the massive health complications and, ironically, the lack of productivity, even before burnout, that was caused by living like that. In between the admiring conversations and social media highlights that I posted, this superwoman was exhausted! The point I want to highlight here is that this dream killer of not putting on your own oxygen mask first tends to work in brilliant partnership with the 'I'll do it when...' mindset. In my case, they both went on to successfully rob me of a significant amount of time when my body finally forced me to slow down.

I'd love for you to honestly assess whether either, or both, of these dream killers are also robbing you in your life? This is the devastating reality for so many mothers who are totally burnt out, or heading that way, while often remaining totally oblivious to how bad things actually are, due to these sneaky dream killers. For what seems like forever, so many mums have had to deal with what often feels like the impossible task of having to take care of everyone and everything in our lives and work.

The pressure to be 'on it, all the time' comes from all around us. Society expects it, family expects it, and, let's be real, a lot of the time we expect it the most ourselves. I have found that, as mums, we are often the hardest on ourselves. Then, as we start working towards unrealistic expectations from ourselves and others, we struggle to juggle it all and end up feeling like twenty-four hours is nowhere near enough to do everything. Time just for ourselves gets reduced in our minds to some sort of luxury 'reward' that we try to fit in when we can find the time, which, let's face it, is rare, or non-existent for some.

So, we continue on with this never-ending cycle until we are forced to stop, like I was.

I really don't want you or any other woman to go through that, so I invite you to commit to putting on your own oxygen mask first, daily, by taking time just for you, come what may, until it becomes as habitual as brushing your teeth. You deserve and quite frankly need this. None of us can pour from an empty cup; we are all much better mums, and can perform better in whatever other roles we get to fulfil, when we take care of ourselves first.

## How exactly do you do this?

I highly recommend carving out time for yourself – 'me time' – regularly, and ideally first thing, before focusing on everyone and everything else. You can use it for self-care, to read, to do whatever you would put under the umbrella of 'taking care of yourself' without even an ounce of guilt. However, more important than whatever it is you likely currently have under that umbrella, my recommendation is for you to use this time to ensure you take care of all of you. By that, I mean your spirit, your soul and your body.

There is so much more to you than the physical body you see in the mirror. When you invest the time to ensure all of you is amazingly well taken care of, you will save time and see that twenty-four hours a day is in fact enough to achieve everything you need to. From this place, it is so much easier to take care of your family and do all the things you need to do, even in this crazy-busy world we live in. When all of you, spirit, soul and body, is well taken care of, you can also more easily become a conduit for innovative solutions that have the potential to not only impact your world, but the world at large to flow through.

When I ask mums how they would take amazing care of themselves if they didn't have so much to juggle, the majority respond by saying something related to taking care of their physical body, whether that's by getting into better physical shape, finally getting that haircut, manicure, massage or whatever it is they have on their self-care wish list. Perhaps you're the same? There's nothing wrong with any of that – I love to do all those things and more for myself, but let me show you how this is nowhere near enough.

Take a moment to think about what taking care of your physical body means to you, especially to ease stress and overwhelm.

Once you have your answer, keep that in mind for a minute as you continue to track with me. Chances are that whatever you just thought of you have done before, right? However, have you noticed that when you managed to fit that thing in before, such as a massage, things felt great for a little while but then, not too long after, those feelings of overwhelm, guilt, worry and stress that can afflict us soon crept back in? That's because although you found a way to take care of some part of your body, there is also your soul and spirit that make up who you are, which are possibly in desperate need of some TLC.

When these parts of you remain uncared for, it makes it so much more difficult to face, and overcome, the monumental challenges that confront us as mothers. Sticking with the flight analogy I used earlier, imagine being on a plane during an emergency that led to a drastic shortage of oxygen on board. The emergency oxygen masks drop as expected, and you pull yours closer to you, but you don't actually put it on. Instead, you frantically try to help everyone around you while struggling desperately to breathe. How long do you think you'll be able to keep that up? That's in effect what we are doing when we neglect to take care of our whole being: spirit, soul and body. Self-care activities that only look after our physical body, while great, are simply not sufficient. They are sort of like pulling the mask closer but not actually putting it on so that we can breathe and function more effectively as we care for others. The effects of such 'rewards' and 'treats', as many mums view them, quickly wear off, and we go back to feeling overwhelmed and like we are failing despite our best efforts. To overcome this, I encourage you to adopt a more holistic self-care regime, one that, in addition to taking care of your physical body, is also focused on helping you nurture the other highly intelligent, influential and invisible parts of yourself. Remember much of you, and everything around you, exists in the unseen realm.

As you nurture these invisible parts of you, the visible life you go on to create and live will be one in which you feel much more empowered and fulfilled as you go for, and achieve, your aligned goals. You will also experience a heightened sense of peace, purpose and productivity, because in addition to being exceptionally well taken care of, you will also be able to more easily take amazing care of everyone and everything you need to, even when you are facing times of uncertainty and crisis.

Before we continue with how you can actually practise holistic self-care, let me share with you how I am defining your spirit, soul and body, so that we are definitely on the same page about them.

The body is fairly obvious; it's what you see in the mirror. This part of you is governed by your five physical senses, which are sight, sound, smell, taste and touch. Depending on what our senses are exposed to, they can lead to us experiencing various feelings linked to the stimuli. For example, if you receive a harsh touch, like a slap to the face, you would feel a multitude of things – very likely the pain of the slap on your face, but perhaps also shock, anger or some other understandable emotion, given what happened. The difference with these secondary feelings is that, unlike the pain on your face, you don't feel them on your physical body, but in your soul.

Ancient wisdom suggests that this part of you is home to your mind, your will and your emotions. One of the most famous Greek philosophers, Plato, also sets out a theory that the soul is divided into three parts in his work *The Republic*. He called them 'logistikon' (mind), 'epithymetikon', which deals with our appetites (or our will), and 'thymoeides' (emotions). Those are the sorts of things that you deal with on a soul level.

Last, but definitely not least, there is your spirit; I like to think of this as the deepest part of you that is not moved by what you sense or feel. I believe it's the part of you that helps you download the powerful internal wisdom I have been talking about throughout this book. This is often wisdom and insight that your rational mind in your soul had no way of knowing, like those moments when you just have a gut feeling about something that is not necessarily based on anything you have seen, heard or felt. When that happens, I believe it is very likely your spirit at work providing you intuition, which I like to think of as tuition from within. If you went on to follow that intuition, the chances are that things worked out well in some way, or you avoided something bad happening. If you ignored it, however, perhaps there were some unfortunate consequences. So many times I have heard people say, 'I should have trusted my gut,' but never once have I heard anyone say, 'I should have trusted my head.' Your spirit is the literal gamechanger for helping you create a life in which you have it all. That is because it can grant you access to so much wisdom that can radically transform your life like little else can, including the other parts of your being. You have heard some of the powerful examples of this from my life story so far. Think back over your own – can you trace your spirit at work downloading life-changing insights that you implemented or ignored? What were the results? Hopefully you can see how powerful this part of you is from even a very quick trip down memory lane.

Whole books could be, and probably have been, written just about these three parts of you, but hopefully these short descriptions help us to have some common understanding as we continue, and help you see why some of the things we treat as self-care fall significantly short of being able to help us take amazing care of ourselves and our families. Most of those activities don't even begin to scratch the surface when we view self-care holistically. That is why, while I strongly encourage you to practise self-care that addresses the needs of your physical body, I actually recommend that you start by focusing on the parts of you that can make the biggest difference: your spirit and soul.

The effects of lack of self-care at the physical body level are clear, with burnout like I suffered being a major risk, and something that's significantly on the rise right now in mums. The effects can be much more devastating on our time and lives when we fail to nurture the spirit and soul. Let's start at the spirit level.

As we face all the difficulties that we can encounter as mums, it is easy in the first instance to look outside of ourselves for a solution, whether that's to the government in our country, the company we work for, the women's conference speakers, other mums, and so on. However, when we do that, we could actually be wasting time and reducing our chances of success.

If governments, companies, mothers' groups and wherever else outside of yourself that you may decide to look for answers could have helped you solve your most pressing issues, they would have done it by now. There is simply no one-size-fits-all, cookie-cutter solution that you can find to any of these challenges that we face as mums. That's not to say you need to figure everything out yourself and not get help from anyone – far from it – but only do so after first taking time to receive tuition from within to be divinely guided to the right helpers and solutions for you, your family and everything else.

The most transformative answers always have, and always will be, within you. You are more powerful than you likely give yourself credit for. When you practise self-care at the spirit level by regularly listening to and accessing what is within you, that is where the radical transformation happens. You will see that you are powerful enough to create a life beyond your wildest dreams, no matter what it looks like now, and no matter what is going on around you. Your spirit can help you access powerful wisdom to empower and guide you every step of the way on your unique journey. This is exactly what I accidently tapped into that night when I stood face to face with that pimp in Soho. It was through my spirit that I heard the voice that told me, 'This is not who you are meant to be, you are meant for so much more.'

Even though this wisdom seemed like complete and utter nonsense based on everything my soul and physical senses were experiencing, I just knew in my gut that it was right, and thankfully I trusted my gut. I can't even begin to calculate how much time and quality of life I would have wasted had I chosen to ignore this deepest part of me and focus on others in that moment. I am so grateful that I accidently chose to practise one of the most powerful forms of self-care that day, and you can start to do this too, if you don't already. It's simple, you just need to regularly take time to listen to, and check in on yourself at the start of and throughout your day, then, crucially, you need to have the courage to follow the guidance you receive.

So many people hear this wisdom from within themselves, but they brush it off, or fail to use it strategically, and then go on to suffer the consequences. I have sadly also made this mistake myself with some decisions, such as when, on one occasion, I agreed to connect and work with a certain individual. Everything looked good on the outside when I reviewed their proposal, so I said yes for fear of losing such a great opportunity, even though my spirit inside me was screaming, 'Say NO!' Not listening to my gut instincts in this case cost me significantly in terms of wasted time, money, other relationships and so much more. It was a complete and utter disaster that took years to recover from.

What could ignoring your spirit cost you? Probably far more than you can even imagine now. I encourage you to minimise and, if possible, eliminate this cost by checking in with and regularly following your intuition when you sense it's leading you, even if it makes no sense at the time. If your spirit is uncared for through being ignored when it's trying to help you, this will negatively impact your time and your life, in the same way as ignoring any other person you are in a relationship with will gradually cause pain. This inward-out approach to life of being guided by your spirit is especially crucial now, given how rapidly the world has changed and continues to change. The places outside ourselves that we used to unsuccessfully look to for solutions are now even less effective, because things are so different, uncertain and unpredictable in this new world.

The women who use this strategy of being guided by their spirit are still able to keep progressing towards creating astonishing lives for themselves and others even during these chaotic times that no one seems to have an adequate frame of reference for. Like you and me, they are women with a lot of responsibilities, and little time to waste on solutions that don't work. They have also found that putting on their own oxygen mask first by checking in with their spirit for guidance is one of the best time- and life-savers there is. So please, make time to do this daily, as I outlined on page 58, in the section on daily success habits.

In a similar manner, caring for your soul – your mind, will and emotions – is critical. What are the things your soul craves? Regularly getting lost in a good book? Having a guilt-free girls' night out? Therapy to deal with trauma or loss? Romance with your partner to keep the spark alive? To discover and start moving towards your purpose? I highly recommend regularly journaling on the question – *What does my soul need right now?*

Whatever it is for you, it is of paramount importance that you put on your own oxygen mask first by making time and space for it by at the very least scheduling it, before continuing with what you are doing for everyone else. When the appointment comes round, treat it as you would an appointment related to one of the most important people in your life, because that is exactly what it is. Many mums, myself included, have been quick to cancel commitments to themselves when the schedule gets busy. Continually doing this is a mistake that will likely later rob you of way more than the time you think you are saving by not doing it. For example, I have seen many women who have had to deal with depression due to loneliness and unaddressed trauma. Ignoring your soul is a costly mistake, and I urge you to avoid this by checking in and giving it the care it needs.

Similarly, check in regularly on what your physical body needs, and give it to yourself. You deserve it; not as a reward for anything you've done, or crossed off your list, but because you are worthy of it and need it. You deserve it simply because you are you, a human that needs to be well looked after to thrive. These are things you can consider as you work on your weekly success schedule as outlined in Chapter 1. Make time as you create your schedule to nurture spirit, soul and body.

Please don't make the mistake I did for years of thinking I was being selfish for wanting to put myself first. As I dealt with the repercussions of a body, soul and spirit that were so done with being neglected, it was the very people I thought I was sacrificing for that suffered the most. Please make time to care for your spirit, soul and body, by listening to each part, and taking steps, however small, to give each part of you what you need. Small steps lead to big results over time.

Let me end with the story of one of my clients, a beautiful mum of three. She had moved from her home country to another and put her own career on hold while having children and supporting her husband in his career. She has incredible musical talent, and her soul was craving being able to step into her purpose of being paid well to make music. Her rational mind told her this was totally unrealistic, given all she had to do to support her husband and kids, and the fact that her career prior to maternity leave was in the very practical and stable medical field.

I helped her work through the advice I gave you above of practising spirit and soul care regularly. As she continued to tap into her internal wisdom and nurture her soul, she went on to create an incredible opportunity for her whole family to move to another city, where both she and her husband are paid extremely well to make music and raise their children in safe and stunning surroundings. This outcome seemed totally impossible when we got started, and it would have been, had she not put on her own oxygen mask first. What opportunities will you create for you and the loved ones in your life when you practise holistic self-care? One of the most selfless things you can do for them is to get started and find out.

## Key takeaways

- For what seems like forever, so many mums have had to deal with what often feels like the impossible task of having to take care of everyone and everything in their lives and work.
- The pressure to be on it, all the time, comes from all around. Society expects it, family expects it and, let's be real, a lot of the time we expect it of ourselves the most.
- None of us can pour from an empty cup; we are all much better mums, and whatever other roles we get to fulfil, when we are taken care of first.
- It is important to put on your mask first by practising 'holistic self-care', which ensures all of your being, spirit, soul and body are well looked after. The effects can be devastating on our time and lives when we fail to nurture all parts of us.
- I highly recommend incorporating holistic self-care practices into your weekly and daily success habits. Make time each day and week to:
  - Care for your spirit by regularly tapping into and following the wisdom you receive from it.
  - Care for your soul by making time to discover what its healthy cravings are and give them to it.
  - Care for your body by doing the same, and ensuring you get adequate rest, exercise and nutrition.
- Schedule time for all these holistic self-care activities. and when the appointments come around, treat them as you would an appointment with one of the most important people in your life, because that is exactly what it is.
- Don't fall prey to the 'I'll do it when...' mindset, which works brilliantly with this dream killer. Not being able to find time

is an excuse that many mums use to not get started. You will never find the time; you will either have to carve it out as I am encouraging you to, or have it taken from you by force when your spirit, soul and body finally have enough of being neglected. I encourage you not to learn the hard way. Carve out time, however small to begin with, to care for your spirit, soul and body, by listening to each part, and taking steps to give each part of you what you need. Small steps lead to big results over time.

# Chapter 6: Not Feeling Good Enough

There is an unfortunate tendency I have noticed in the vast majority of the mums I have worked with. No matter what country we are from, or what we do for a living, at some point most of us have felt like we are not good enough in some way or another. We have felt as if all our past successes were flukes, and that we will soon be exposed for the impostors that we truly are. Whether we are facing something work-related, trying to take care of ourselves, our family or other items on our to-do lists, many of us have experienced not feeling as confident as we would like, and worrying that we may not measure up. Can you relate to any of this?

If so, the dream killer of not feeling good enough is very likely at work in your life, robbing you of time and so much more. This sneaky dream killer causes us to waste time thinking through self-doubt-saturated questions and thoughts like, *What if I don't succeed with this job? It's bigger than anything I have ever done!* Maybe for you, as it is for countless women I have worked with, it's thoughts like, *I am a terrible mum, especially compared to that other perfect super mum!*

On and on, we waste time wondering in our own words and ways whether we have what it takes to succeed. This is especially stressful when we are navigating the previously unchartered and terrifying waters to which our quest to 'have it all' has led us. The temptation to give up or quit then becomes almost overwhelming. If you are tempted to give up on your dream of creating and living your best, most incredible life due to this, please don't.

## How I discovered this dream killer

I came face to face with this crippling dream killer of not feeling good enough when I started a new job. I was so excited about the incredible opportunity to work in the leadership team of a business that was having tremendous impact and success around the world. I kicked off my tenure in the role by travelling for a week-long business trip to meet my predecessor for a handover. As we worked through the intense and packed schedule, which included talking about the people, processes, protocol and much else within the role, I started to feel extremely nervous that perhaps I was not the right person for the job.

I had read an article prior to applying that was aimed at encouraging women to be more ambitious with their careers. It suggested that, on average, women look at a job description and expect to be able to do close to one hundred per cent of the role before applying. The article compared that to men who, on average, felt comfortable applying if they believed they could do at least fifty per cent of the role. The article concluded that this was hurting women's careers, and that, if we aspired to progress, we ought to learn from men in this regard. So that's what I resolved to do.

With this particular role, on reading the job description I felt I could do at least seventy-five per cent of the role, and so I applied, against my normal tendencies. To my delight, I managed to convince the hiring executives that I was indeed the woman for the job. However, as I sat in the airport waiting to fly home after the handover week, with a journal full of notes and a pounding headache from massive information overload, I wondered whether I'd be able to do even ten per cent of the role! I feared that I, and the hiring executives, had all made a terrible mistake, and wondered how long it would be before I was found out and fired. Thankfully, it was the weekend, so I figured I had at least a few days of employment left before the new week. For the next two nights I lay awake in bed, tossing and turning, worrying about what to do for hours on end, and getting nowhere.

By Sunday night I was super stressed, and filled with dread at the prospect of the new week; the week where I was certain I would be discovered and exposed as an impostor. I didn't know what else to do, so aloud I said something along the lines of, 'I really hope some sort of overnight miracle, bringing ideas on how to handle this situation, comes to me by the morning.' It felt as though a weight had lifted off me after I said that, and I was finally able to fall asleep.

The next morning, I woke up strangely calm for the first time in days, a feeling that I welcomed gratefully after so many days of anxiety. Given my experiences in life, one of my strengths is being able to comfortably chat to and connect with almost anyone, right from the homeless person many people would walk quickly past or ignore on the street, all the way up to the leader of any nation, I'd imagine! When I have an opportunity to chat, I have learnt how to really connect with a wide variety of people across cultures to have a mutually enjoyable conversation. The idea that came to me was why didn't I start by arranging to chat one-on-one with all my peers on the leadership team?

So, that's what I decided to do to get started in my role. I scheduled meetings with key stakeholders, starting with the principal global leader and including the regional leaders and any others who would work with me directly. During the meetings, in addition to ensuring I connected with them all in positive ways, I got clear on what their goals and aspirations were, what success looked like for them in terms of how I did my role; what worked for them in the past with my predecessors, and what didn't. With these viewpoints I got a clear definition of what a successful expected outcome looked like for me in the role, and how I could help others to be even more successful than they already were. I then went on to redesign the role and work processes to utilise other strengths I knew I possessed, such as being great at public speaking, writing and simplifying complex issues. Playing to my strengths, I not only achieved but also exceeded the expectations for success. The feedback was incredible at every single appraisal I had, much to my relief!

## Overcoming this dream killer

So, how exactly do you invest time to overcome this dream killer? I found the answer as I looked more closely at my experience above, and those of the hundreds of women I have coached and spoken to about this. Typically, when we are feeling like we are not good enough, we are usually comparing ourselves to someone else – either directly or at some subconscious level. We check out how others work, look, dress or take care of their kids, and we fear that we will never be good enough to measure up.

The sad truth is this: when we think this, we are one hundred per cent right, because we never will be good enough – that is, if we keep comparing ourselves to others and trying to do things the way they do. Theodore Roosevelt, the 26th President of the United States of America, is credited with the famous quote: 'Comparison is the thief of joy.' I couldn't agree more, and I would add to this that comparison is also a pretty good thief of time, and your most incredible life.

No matter what you think, or how you feel, you are enough – and you are definitely good enough, just as you are right now. In fact, you are a unique one-of-a-kind masterpiece – even with whatever flaws, weaknesses, imperfections and anything else you think disqualifies you from being good enough. The undeniable truth is that you are a genius when you are simply who you are meant to be. There is no one in the world better at that, not one single person. It is a real gamechanger when you fully embrace who you are meant to be, by discovering and leveraging your unique strengths.

Unless you are trying to do something like brain surgery, that requires following instructions down to the last detail, always remember that you have your own individual strengths and style that you can leverage to your advantage with most things that you get to do. When you discover and begin to leverage these consistently, not feeling good enough will become a thing of the past. In its place, you will feel confidence, as you deliver exceptional results against your goals, at home, work, with your kids, and everywhere else as well.

To help you do this I developed the 6C Confidence Checklist. It's a simple, step-by-step checklist that you can use to boost your confidence by discovering, and using your unique strengths to your advantage, so that you no longer waste precious time that could be better invested by feeling like you are not good enough as you consider what you need to do for yourself and for your family.

## The 6C Confidence Checklist

If you find yourself lacking in confidence, or feeling like you are not good enough to achieve some aspect of your dream of having it all, I encourage you to invest some time in going through the checklist below. It will lead to the incredible return on investment of getting you right back on track to efficiently creating and living the fabulous life you're meant to manifest.

### Clarify the desired outcome

A lot of mums get stuck when trying to reach their ambitious goals because they are focused on the 'how' instead of the 'whats'. For example, during the handover for the job I told you about, I got so stressed by worrying how in the world I would be able to do this job in the way that one guy was explaining it to me. He might as well have been speaking Greek – which I definitely don't understand! A better approach, which I thankfully discovered later, was to pause on focusing on the 'how' for a while, and to instead focus on two 'whats' that would help me clarify the desired outcome.

As you tackle your goals, don't waste time worrying how you will complete them initially. Instead, I invite you to clarify the desired outcome by considering two 'what' questions:

'What am I trying to achieve by doing this?'

And,

'What do I need to see to know that I have been successful?'

For example, in my life as a mum, rather than wasting time

feeling crap that I am not able to bake cakes and desserts anywhere near as well as my other mum friends for my kids' birthday parties, I could instead clarify the desired outcome as follows with the two answers to the 'what' questions above:

1. What I am trying to achieve is to joyfully throw amazing birthday parties, full of memorable moments for my children.
2. To know I have been successful at achieving this, I would need to see that I am not stressed by the preparations, and that we have things in place to create those wonderful memories, including incredible cakes and desserts the kids would love.

As you can see, at this stage I am not giving any thought to *how* we will achieve any of this, just what needs to happen, and be put in place, and how I would like to feel through it all. In a similar way, for your own goals, you want to separate the 'hows' from the 'whats' in the first instance.

## Clarify your strengths

In other words, work out what you are amazing at. As I alluded to before, the more you are clear on, and the more you begin to use these strengths to complete your to-dos, the better the results you will see. You will also achieve a much greater level of efficiency as you create those results. Being more efficient will naturally help you create even more time to use for yourself or whatever else you want to do. There are many ways you can get clear on your strengths, so feel free to get creative with this, but let me share with you three of my favourite ways to help you get started, or to give you more ideas.

### 1. Ask people close to you what you're good at

One of the first things mums say when I ask them to tell me their strengths or what they are amazing at is, 'I don't know,' or 'I can't think of anything.' We often think that the things that make us brilliant are no big deal; surely everyone can do them, right? Wrong! We feel that because some things come easily to us they are nothing special, and definitely not worth 'bragging' about. That couldn't be further from the truth. There are few things more special than creating a life in which we use processes that come easily to us to get stuff done wherever possible. There are already so many extremely difficult things that are out of our control that we have to face as mums, so I am all for making what we can control easy; and we do that by leveraging what comes naturally to us where possible. What things come naturally to you may not be so obvious to you, but chances are they will be to those who are around you, so ask them. You may be surprised at what you find out from trusted loved ones in this way. One of my clients in the past even put out a post on Facebook inviting her hundreds of friends who knew her quite well to tell her what they see as her strengths. She was blown away by the dozens of responses that pointed out clear areas of genius in herself that she had been taking for granted.

### 2. Acknowledge and review past successes

This is another great way to clarify what strengths you have so that you can use them to your benefit. What are some of your past personal or professional successes that you are proud of, or that even surprised you? What strengths helped you achieve them? As mentioned earlier, one of my strengths is public speaking, but I never even realised it until I reviewed a surprising past success. Growing up, I was a shy, introverted child who spent most of her childhood years reading one book or another. The thought of getting up to speak in front of anyone was absolutely mortifying. However, during a visit to Nigeria as an adult, shortly after I had graduated from Cambridge, one of my aunts suggested that I give a motivational speech to the youth group she was in charge of leading. This was the last thing in the world I wanted to do, so I vehemently refused. She kept asking the whole week leading up to Sunday, the day the speech was meant to happen. I refused repeatedly, getting more and more annoyed that she wouldn't let it go. The day finally arrived and she somehow persuaded me to come along to at least meet the young people, and I agreed, figuring there was no harm in seeing how she ran the group and saying hello. There was about a hundred of them, and after a few small-talk conversations I could feel my energy levels draining, so the introvert in me found a quiet spot at the back of the room to regain some of it on my own while I watched how their meeting would unfold.

Much to my horror, after I had been sitting down for barely a few minutes, my aunt went on to make a grand introduction of me as their motivational speaker for the day. Everyone started applauding, cheering and looking in my direction, expecting me to walk up to the podium. I hoped and prayed the ground would open up and swallow me. When it didn't, my eyes darted across the room, weighing up my options. I could run for the door and just leave, but there were too many people in the way, plus I was wearing heels! *What if I pretended to faint?* I wondered. *Maybe that could work?*

I weighed up one crazy option after another in my mind for what felt like an eternity as over a hundred pairs of eyes remained glued on me, excitedly willing me to come up and inspire them. When I couldn't come up with a viable escape plan, I had no option but to stand up and walk slowly to the front. I gave my aunt a look that clearly conveyed my threat to deal with her later, big time. I had no idea what I would talk to them about for thirty long minutes, so in my mind I kept asking, *What on earth do I tell them that would be helpful?* as I dragged myself slowly to the front. When I got there, what came to mind was something I had read just before flying to Nigeria that I had found really enlightening. The basic gist of the text is that we always have a choice no matter how things look, and that it is important to make the right choice for good, whatever the situation, not just for us, but also for the benefit of those around us.

I decided to start my motivational speech by telling them about what I had read and how it impacted me. I then just spoke from my heart about making good versus bad choices based on my experiences. To my utter shock and amazement, it went brilliantly, and I talked for well over the thirty minutes allocated, and no one minded. In their words, it was a 'spectacular' speech. They laughed, cried and got so much from the whole thing. I was blown away. In reviewing this surprising success, I discovered my strength for public speaking, which I have continued to hone and use wherever possible. I still often feel the nerves I felt that day before I give a speech, but I deal with those by focusing on the desired outcome, which is almost always to positively impact those listening. I even created a little acronym I'M AMAZING to help with this:

**It**'s
**M**ore
**A**bout
**M**y
**A**udience than Me
**Z**ero
**I**n on their
**N**eeds and
**G**oals

So any time I feel nervous or not good enough using this strength, I remember I'M AMAZING! If you ever have to speak to an audience, feel free to use this too.

What about you? What clues do your successes, expected or unexpected, leave about what your strengths are? Get clear on those and figure out how to get more comfortable using them like I did, if applicable, so you can leverage them where it makes sense for new challenges.

### 3. Use assessments

The final way to clarify your strengths that I want to touch on here is to use assessments, if possible. There are always many great assessments on the market that you can use to get a greater understanding of your strengths and instinctive ways of taking action. They can be especially powerful for you in terms of helping you drop the Mum guilt and frustration you carry as you handle your to-dos in ways that make sense for how you are uniquely wired. For example, sticking with my public-speaking strength, colleagues and others around me quickly realised this is an area of strength for me, so I was invited to speak quite often. A lot of the time I would use presentation slides, as that was the norm, but when it came to preparing the slides and actual presentation, every time I tried to do this well in advance of the actual speech, I would find myself feeling unmotivated and would end up wasting time procrastinating by going on social media, or getting a snack or drink that I didn't really need. I would then feel terrible for ruining my healthy eating goals and wasting time when I had so many other things to do that I could have used the time for. Typically, the day before I was meant to give the talk, I would then somehow miraculously manage to get it all done to a high standard just in time. This happened over and over again – feeling unmotivated, leading to procrastination and overeating, then feeling guilt and regret, to finally getting it done brilliantly at the last minute. It was only when I took an assessment designed to highlight your strengths and how you instinctively take action best that I understood what was going on.

Through my assessment results, I found out that I am driven and motivated by deadlines. So, when I was trying to prepare well in advance for my presentations, I was working in exact opposition to how I am naturally wired to work best, hence ending up wasting time and feeling unmotivated. The way each of us is uniquely wired causes us to find that some activities and ways of working give us energy, while others drain our energy. If you regularly work against your own unique wiring it will likely feel like one big, confidence-sapping energy drain. You may then go on to incorrectly attribute this to feeling unmotivated, and not being good enough to succeed at the task at hand. If you are feeling anything like this, it may not be the case that you are unmotivated, or not good enough, it could simply be that you are going about things the wrong way for your own unique wiring. It is therefore extremely helpful to use assessments to understand yourself better, so you can make changes to how you approach your to-dos accordingly.

## Create the best process to achieve the desired outcome

This next C in our Confidence Checklist is pretty straightforward. All you need to do is consider what you are good at and how you are wired, then figure out the best way to complete your to-dos based on that. Take the example of preparing for speeches that I shared above; I now know not to bother wasting my time and energy too far in advance on preparation. The best process for me is to plan my prep for the speech close to the deadline, which gives me even more energy to do an excellent job of actually delivering the speech. If I am collaborating with others and can't leave things to the last minute, I make sure to create a process with built-in deadlines along the way, such as meetings with collaborators to review and practise. These help me feel accountable to others, another thing I am wired to be motivated by. Such mini deadlines also have the same energy-giving motivating effect that the main deadline has on me.

## Communicate clearly and confidently

It's tremendously important to get on the same page with others if the to-do list you are working on affects them in any way, so they know what you are doing, and what to expect. This is especially important if you have created a completely different process to what they are used to in the previous step. Let them know the desired outcome you are working towards so that you are both agreed on what success looks like. Tweak the definition of success if necessary until you are both in agreement, then let them know how you intend to achieve this by leveraging your strengths. Try to be confident and unapologetic as you share your reasoning. If relevant, agree to future meetings to get their feedback or whatever other input is needed. You want to leave these conversations with all parties being clear on what is being done, how, by when, and what to expect along the way, so that there are no surprises for anyone. One of the biggest issues I see causing mums stress in their work and personal lives is unfulfilled expectations, mostly due to one of the parties not even being aware there was an expectation of them in the first place. The resulting fallout often knocks our confidence and perpetuates that feeling that we are somehow not good enough. Use this opportunity of clear, confident communication to avoid that.

## Complete the process from, not for, success

The first part, 'complete the process', is fairly obvious; take action on the thing you need to do. To do it from, not for, success means that we are much more intentional in our approach. When we do something intentionally, it's not just the action that matters; it's our whole attitude, our body language, what we think, say and feel, as we do it that determines whether it is a truly successful action or not. To illustrate, think through the following two scenarios with one of your children in mind, if they are old enough to tidy their room. If not, think of another child who is old enough. You politely ask the child to go and clean their room, which was a terrible mess when you went in there earlier. In the first scenario, the child ignores you, so you need to repeat yourself so many times that you end up getting annoyed, issuing a relevant consequence like a time out, or taking away some of their technology privileges, before they finally agree to do it. They complete the job feeling annoyed, dragging their feet, rolling their eyes, and mumbling all sorts of things under their breath at, and about you, causing a tense atmosphere that you could cut with a knife. By the time the room is clean, it's nowhere near as good as you'd hoped, but you can't be bothered to keep dealing with the drama so you move on, feeling annoyed.

In the second scenario, when you ask the child to clean their room, the first time you ask he or she gets up cheerfully and says, 'Yes, I'd be glad to, I'm so sorry it was such a mess.' They then proceed to cheerfully get on with the task at hand with a great attitude, checking with you from time to time about whether things are coming along in line with your expectations. By the time the room is clean, it's evident they have done a brilliant job. Again, it may not be as perfect as if you had done it, but you move on happily thanks to the good atmosphere in the house throughout the experience.

In both scenarios, the room ended up clean, but which scenario was truly successful? Clearly the second one. The key difference between the two scenarios was how the child responded to and approached the request to tidy their room – success in the second scenario was already guaranteed before the child even started cleaning, because as I mentioned before, it's not just *what* we do that creates success, but also things like our attitude, body language, what we think and what we say as we do it that also play a huge role. Embarking on a task reluctantly and begrudgingly and feeling resentful is never going to result in the best outcome.

To complete your to-dos from, not for, success, I invite you to start completing them as the future you who has already success- fully created the vision you hope to achieve. As much as you can, do things as if you are already successfully her – think like her, talk like her, act like her as much as you can, as you go about whatever it is you need to do. It may feel awkward and as though you are faking it at first, but I promise you, as you see more and more success, it will become second nature.

To help with this, ask yourself questions like, *How would I think, talk or act if I were already that successful mother that has it all*? Then complete your tasks that way as much as possible. I see so many mums derail their best efforts with trying to thrive in work and life by saying the exact opposite of what they really want. They say things like, 'I always feel overwhelmed!' when their actual goal is to create a sense of harmony between their professional and personal lives. They then go on to create perpetual cycles of burnout-inducing overwhelm with their words.

I'm not denying that we get negative thoughts and feelings that are satisfying to vent and rant about – I'm almost certain that we all do. But we don't have to roll out the red carpet and entertain those thoughts and feelings. That leads to us literally cursing ourselves by saying them aloud. Our words have power. I can't stress enough what a truth this is; seemingly harmless statements I hear mums say all the time, like, 'These kids are driving me crazy!' or 'I'm so sick and tired of this!' are actually extremely harmful. When someone says things like 'Silly me!' or 'I'm so stupid,' when their desire is actually to have their brilliance and contribution be recognised by others in order to get more flexibility and progress in their career, they are coming into agreement with the dream killer of not feeling good enough. Agreement is powerful, so this keeps them stuck. Watch what you say, and make sure you're not unintentionally cursing yourself with your words. The power of words and agreement works both ways, so be sure to affirm and create success for yourself with your words – we create what we say. I have a powerful practice of interrupting any negative thoughts or feelings I catch myself entertaining with a strong positive affirmation that I'll say aloud. You can't keep thinking negatively if you start speaking positive words and affirmations to yourself – try it. The good news is that as you continue to do this, you will eventually create the positive vision you keep speaking.

My life has been a powerful testament to that since birth. In Nigeria, where I was born, names are a big deal. They are often selected to reflect the situation the child was born into and are said to significantly affect the child's destiny. My maternal grandmother suggested my parents name me Nkiruka, which literally means 'the future is greater', and thankfully they did. I began to use my middle name Maxine after I moved to the UK in the early 1990s, as I figured it would be easier for people in Britain to pronounce, but I am, and will always be, Nkiruka – the Future is Greater. That name has definitely gone on to affect my destiny significantly; every time I was called by my name growing up, someone was literally saying 'the future is greater' over me. I believe the power of those words being spoken over me time and time again are the reason I am who I am today. I believe that it was partly as a result of these words being spoken over me for so many years that when I hit rock bottom, and was faced with the option of continuing to ruin my life further, I was able to hear and receive that wisdom that drove me to seek out an alternative life for myself.

Having 'the future is greater' spoken over me countless times has also led to one of my greatest skills: the ability to take whatever raw hand I have been dealt and make a masterpiece out of it. I love helping my clients, readers and everyone I encounter to do exactly the same. No matter what is happening in my life, I remain the eternal optimist, and inevitably I then create something much greater. I believe a lot of that has to do with my name Nkiruka; the power of those words is still creating good in my life, and now the lives of so many others around the world through my work. I hope to add yours too.

So always remember that your words have power. Unless you would like to see the words you are saying manifested in your life, don't say them; watch them carefully and make sure they align with the person you desire to become in the future. By thinking about yourself as if you already have it all, you will find that it affects how you feel, what you say and how you act, all of which will increase the level of success you create.

As you create those new levels of success, don't be tempted to overlook the sixth and final C in the checklist, as I and a lot of other mums have a tendency to do.

## Celebrate how far you've come

Celebrate not just what you have achieved – although celebrating that is always great – but the actual progress you have made, too. In my case, with the job I was feeling like an impostor in, this meant celebrating that I went from feeling like I'd barely be able to do ten per cent of the role to delivering well over one hundred per cent when I exceeded all expectations.

This focus on progress made, rather than just the outcome, is important for a couple of reasons. First, on a very obvious level, it strengthens our confidence when we pause, acknowledge our growth and our development and forward momentum towards our goals. But, more importantly, this focus on our progress rather than the outcome is an extremely powerful technique and habit to master in this volatile, complex and uncertain world we live in. While things remain like this, our past accomplishments may often pale in comparison to the new challenges we will have to face. If we just stop to celebrate the successful outcome we achieved in the past or, worse yet, move on without acknowledging or celebrating in any way, I can tell you from personal experience that it is much more difficult to find the courage and confidence within oneself in the future to slay the necessary giants to claim your dreams and destiny. You are instead tempted to waste time worrying, fretting and doubting your abilities, and as a result you might never try to do the thing in front of you that could be your personal key to overcoming the financial or quality of life penalty of motherhood.

Since I started focusing more on the journey, I began to see, applaud and trust the woman I needed to become in the process of hitting my goal. This was such a gamechanger for me. Think of someone else in your life who you admire, and who you have observed time and time again rising to the challenge and giving it their all. Your trust and confidence in their ability to rise to new, even unprecedented, challenges increases with each time you see them do it, right? In the same way, give yourself the gift of regularly filling up the trust and confidence bank of your abilities by celebrating how far you have come before you move on.

Regarding what you do to celebrate, there are no rules! It can be big, small or even free, based on what resources you have available. The most important thing is that it is tailored to you, and that it's something you love. There have been times when my celebrations have been as simple as a candlelit bubble bath during which I play relaxing music and force myself to stop the usual

NOT FEELING GOOD ENOUGH

worry that there is something more important that I need to be doing. Instead, I meditate and mentally go through the success in my mind, seeing how far I have come and who I have become; then I mentally pat myself on the back before I get out. I feel this action helps to cement it all in my subconscious in a powerful way that helps me be more confident and courageous in the future. Other times, I have had higher-budget celebrations, like buying myself a stunning watch when I successfully made the switch from employee to entrepreneur. In this case, I felt a visible reminder was appropriate to celebrate how far I had come from being the woman literally shaking with terror when I first sensed the desire to move from what felt like the security of a job into the uncertain world of full-time entrepreneurship.

The fact that I went from that place of fear to becoming the woman who built a team and multiplied her corporate salary many times over was so worth celebrating. I chose the watch because I know from reading the book *The 5 Love Languages* by Gary Chapman that my primary love language is to receive lovely gifts, so I gave myself an incredible one. You may want to check out that book to learn about all the love languages, and see what your primary one is. I believe it will help the most important relation-ships in your life tremendously, especially the one with yourself, as you learn to love yourself and celebrate how far you've come in ways that are truly meaningful to you.

There you have it, my 6C Confidence Checklist. I invite you to begin to use this process to overcome the dream killer of not feeling good enough. My clients and I have had amazing success with this. Deliberately designing how we do things based on our unique strengths has led to incredible levels of efficiency and effectiveness that freed up even more time for us to do things like take that relaxing and celebratory bath, or some other helpful, stress-relieving, holistic self-care activity that we previously didn't have time to even think about.

You can use this checklist in any area of your life, not just work. For instance, many lovely and well-meaning family and friends have offered to teach me how to bake so my kids can have lovely birthday cakes and fresh homemade bread. The old me would have immediately agreed to it and signed up to learn to bake like a 'good mum', then felt miserable, or said no and felt guilty. There is nothing wrong with baking if you enjoy it and are good at that sort of thing. However, the new me, who has been tackling to-dos with this 6C Confidence Checklist for some time, can unashamedly and unapologetically admit that I have zero interest in learning to bake for my family. I am terrible at baking and find things like that way too stressful. The last time I baked anything was a birthday cake for one of my friends at university, and even though it came from a pre-packaged cake mix box with clear instructions, I still managed to screw it up. It ended up as a rock-hard mess that looked totally ridiculous. Everyone laughed when they saw it and nearly cracked their teeth trying to eat it. Baking is not one of my strengths. So, with birthday cakes or anything else, I go through the 6C Confidence Checklist, starting with clarifying the desired outcome. Following the rest of the steps, that is exactly what I go on to achieve.

Just because something has to be done, it doesn't mean it has to be done *by me*. The moral of all of this is: you are good enough, and you will always be good enough when you do you by uncovering and leveraging your superpowers to your advantage. So please, whatever you do, do you.

## Key takeaways

- So many of us waste time feeling not good enough or confident enough to go for and reach our goals.
- When we feel like this, we are often comparing ourselves to someone else, either directly or at some subconscious level.
- To overcome this, invest some of your time in following my 6C Confidence Checklist, which is a way to discover and use your unique strengths to your advantage. You are a genius when you 'do you' in this way.
- The 6C Confidence Checklist is:
  1. *Clarify the desired outcome*
  2. *Clarify your strengths*
  3. *Create the best process to achieve the desired outcome*
  4. *Communicate clearly and confidently*
  5. *Complete the process from, not for, success*
  6. *Celebrate how far you've come*

# Chapter 7: Life Just Isn't Fair

When was the last time you experienced a situation that was totally unfair? If you're anything like most of the mothers I have worked with, the answer is sadly likely to be quite recently. This dream killer is long-standing, prevalent and highly effective in its work of robbing us of time, as well as so much more that we hope for in life. For centuries, women and other diverse groups have been held back from personal and collective progress by situations and obstacles that are simply not fair. From the very highest levels of society, through to the places we work and right down to our individual lives, women are struggling to catch up with men, and we often trip up over systemic hurdles on the way.

I can certainly relate to this. I was at a stage in my career where I felt unstoppable, as though I could be, do and achieve anything I wanted. That was until my progress was unexpectedly and abruptly halted by a totally unfair situation.

I had started a new job and was doing my best to not only deliver the high standard of work that was expected, but to also innovate and improve the role based on my strengths and interests. The feedback I had received from the managing director, as well as other leaders on the team, was that my work was outstanding, and I had revolutionised the role. I was thrilled, and thought that, based on this ongoing phenomenal feedback, I was well within my rights to ask for a promotion. As I looked into it to make my case, I discovered that the individuals who held the role before me, all of whom happened to be white men, were actually on a higher level than me when they were doing the very same job.

I was quite annoyed by this, as in a fair world I should really have been promoted to be the same level as them when I was recruited into the role a couple of years back, but for whatever reason, this was not done. All that aside, I figured that, based on the glowing feedback I had consistently received about my radical improvement and transformation of the role since, I could comfortably make the case to be promoted above where they had been. However, as I didn't think it was possible to be promoted two levels at the same time, I asked to simply be promoted to the same level that my predecessors had been on. To my utter shock, this was refused. When I asked why, I was given the ridiculous reason that the job had always been a lower-level role, it was just a coincidence that the men that were in it before me were accidently at a higher level than the role itself for close to a decade before I took over. I shared the feedback that I had received, that I had improved things significantly, and asked whether that made me eligible for an increase in level. Apparently not. I went on to get one unfounded and nonsensical excuse after another as to why a promotion was not possible. I wondered if the situation would have been the same if it had been a white man asking for promotion to the same level that his black female predecessors had been on after he had radically innovated in the role. Very likely not.

I felt angry, disgusted and victimised. I wanted more than

anything to keep progressing with my career so that I could keep increasing my impact, but this situation seemed to have thrown a spanner right into the works. I remained in this livid state for about a week or so, until I came to my senses and remembered the truth: that these people, or anyone else for that matter, would only be able to hold me back if I let them. I recalled when I had been told by that pimp and others all those years ago that I would never amount to anything worthwhile. Back then, they were simply stating the truth based on the mess they could clearly see I had got myself into.

I thought to myself, *If I was able to rise above justifiable limits others tried to place on me then, how much more could I achieve now?* In this totally unfair situation, where the only basis for trying to limit me was their own bias or whatever they wanted to dress it up as. I decided there and then that they didn't get to decide whether I progressed or not.

I started to think through how I could continue to progress in my career anyway. I wondered whether I should get back at them by getting another job with a competitor, or anything else that would make them sorry that they had messed with me. As I cooked up potential plans for revenge, I knew in my gut that none of it felt right. I have always wanted to feel excited, and as if I am living out my purpose in my career, but as I planned my next move, it felt vindictive and spiteful, which are definitely not words I would want to associate with my career. There was no joy or flow in anything, and creative ideas that normally came to me organically as I solved problems weren't forthcoming. I felt so stuck.

As I took a moment to check in with myself and see what this was about, it became clear to me that I needed to forgive the people who I felt were blocking my progress. The anger that I was harbouring towards them was impacting me and my ability to progress. One of my mentors once told me that a lack of forgiveness is like drinking poison and hoping the other person dies. I recalled this advice, and while it annoyed me – because my bosses didn't deserve forgiveness, in my opinion – it made a lot of sense based on how I was feeling. It would have been easier to forgive them if they had apologised or at least admitted that they were wrong, but they hadn't. I finally decided to forgive anyway, more for myself than for them. This was a gamechanger, as it was like a heavy load lifted off me, and soon ideas started flowing again.

I began to regain my amazing insights on how to continue to work with excellence in that same role, and more ideas flowed of what a truly fulfilling career vision was for me. It was clear as the picture came to me: I could not be in that company to fulfil my true calling and purpose.

Realising that, I was then able to focus on the right things, which led to me eventually leaving that company on really good terms, with incredible skills that proved to be highly lucrative assets when I went on to start my business later.

As I reflect on the brilliant clients I have often had the opportunity to work with, and the impact that my work has had on them, their families and communities, I am honestly extremely grateful that I experienced that discrimination. It was clearly very painful at the time, but having transformed that pain to power, and then purpose, I now view that setback as a genuine set-up for my true purpose and fulfilment to be unleashed. That is what I want more than anything for you, too: to transform your pain arising from any unfair situations you may be facing into great power and purpose that will not only positively impact your world, but the world at large, if you so wish it.

## Overcoming this dream killer

When we consider our workplaces, the systemic set-up is far from conducive to equality. Many measures of success and catalysts for progress have tended to favour white men.

Thankfully, lots of organisations now understand the importance and great business sense of creating diverse and inclusive workplaces, and are therefore investing in this. This investment is leading to some progress being made towards gender parity, albeit painfully slowly. There are also those who unfairly discriminate against women, ethnic minorities and other diverse groups, both in and out of work, due to their unconscious or overt bias, which fuels microaggressions and other discriminatory words and actions.

Many mums have suffered the unfairness of unconscious bias that can significantly hinder their progress. For example, a manager does not put forward a high-performing female leader for an incredible opportunity or promotion because he assumes that it might be too much for her as she recently had a baby, without ever checking with the employee herself. Those from minority backgrounds have been victims of outright bias and racism that leads to physical, verbal or other abuse. This has been heartbreaking to experience personally and to witness through others' accounts.

Unfair double standards are also rampant and can threaten to hinder our progress, like the man who powerfully exerts his point and is applauded as a confident leader, while the woman doing the exact same thing is labelled and viewed as aggressive or angry.

Characteristics that are more often displayed in mothers, such as kindness and empathy, have been historically viewed as signs of weakness, and definitely not the traits an effective leader should be exhibiting. One extremely capable and accomplished professional mother I worked with was once told that she was 'too nice' to be promoted to the next level.

To make matters even more challenging for us, there are also the basic physiological differences between men and women that could set us at a disadvantage compared to our male peers. For example, I have spoken with many women throughout my career who felt they were doing quite well keeping up with their male colleagues, until they got pregnant. The sheer exhaustion they faced in the first trimester started to highlight the many physical differences between women and men. Then there's the time off to have the baby, the all-consuming task of breastfeeding, should you choose to feed your baby that way, and so much else that feels so unfair and slows our progress towards our goals when compared to men.

I could go on, because, sadly, in this world in which many systemic issues and outdated workplace structures remain, women face so many unfair obstacles. The majority of women have faced some sort of discrimination, and it's even more prevalent among women of colour. You may even be able to add more unfair situations that you've faced to the above, because the unfortunate truth is, life can be so challenging and unfair at times due to no fault of our own, when people and situations seem to throw a spanner in the works of our progress.

Depending on the particular situation and how devastating its effect, it can lead to deep hurt that robs us of time and ultimately holds us back from our destiny when we don't deal with it in an empowered way. This dream killer is especially brutal because it can rob us twice. Not only does the unfair situation waste our time when we encounter it by slowing progress to our goals, how we respond or react to it can further exacerbate matters.

I see this double blow affecting so many mums, and therefore I thought it was important to include a strategy in this book on how to deal with it. If you are dreaming as big as I hope you are in your quest to have it all, there are likely to be some glass or even concrete ceilings to contend with as you rise towards realising your vision.

## The Triple F Formula

So, how do you stop life's unfair situations from wasting your time, so that you can reach your goals, however ambitious they are? You start by resisting the urge to make any form of kneejerk reaction to the injustice. This typically causes you to waste a lot of time in a terrible mood; time that could be better invested making joyful progress towards the plans you have for your life and your family. When you find yourself facing any sort of unfair situation, instead of reacting, I invite you to respond by investing some time to implement my spirit- and soul-nurturing Triple F Formula.

Having taken numerous other women through the same three-step process since my own experience of painful discrimination, I am confident that investing time to implement this strategy will also empower you to transform the pain caused by whatever unfair situation you are facing into power and then a purpose that radically transforms your life, and the lives of others. I truly believe it can help you overcome any situation that seems unfair, including those where others' unfair words or discrimination attempt to hold you back. Implementing the formula involves changing your thoughts and actions based on three F words – beyond the F word you may have initially thought of when you encountered the unfair situation!

## Faith

The first word I invite you to consider in the Triple F Formula is *Faith*. By this I mean, if people ever try to discriminate against you for your gender, race or anything else, or you face other injustices, have unshakeable faith that they cannot and will not succeed in holding you back from your destiny. One of the synonyms for faith is belief, so the above can also be rewritten to state that if people ever try to discriminate against you, have the unshakeable belief that they cannot and will not succeed in holding you back from your destiny.

I've already shared the quote from Henry Ford, which I love: 'Whether you think you can, or you think you can't, you're right.' I have found that to be so true – our beliefs are powerful! I have also found that you can apply the same thing to this situation; whether you believe people or situations can hold you back, or you believe that they can never hold you back, you're right.

I totally understand there are a lot of evil people and unfair situations, but the truth is, nothing and no one can hold us back indefinitely from our purpose and destiny unless we let them. I'm not denying that there are huge injustices and systemic issues to contend with – there are – but they will only be overcome by those of us who take a firm stand for the vision and purpose in our hearts, with unshakeable faith that no evil or injustice can ever stop us. My life has taught me that people's actions and other unfair situations can make me become a victim, but whether I stay a victim is entirely my choice, and in my power to control, no matter the circumstances. I have made the decision that I am unavailable to remain a victim to anyone or anything!

When we take a stand with firm conviction that even if others hurt or delay us they cannot ultimately stop us, that's where we begin to see breakthrough for ourselves, and others. There are so many examples of people enacting this throughout history. Think of Harriet Tubman, who refused to let the fact that she was born a slave limit the dream she had in her heart of freedom for her and so many others. In his 1964 speech, Nelson Mandela said, 'I have fought against white domination, and I have fought against black domination. I have cherished the ideal of a democratic and free society in which all persons live together in harmony and with equal opportunities. It is an ideal which I hope to live for and to achieve.' This ideal looked totally impossible when he said it, but he went on to achieve the seemingly unimaginable feat of serving as the President of South Africa with that mission at the very core of his leadership and legacy. Similarly, members of the Women's Social and Political Union, also known as the Suffragettes, refused to settle for being thought of and treated as second-class citizens in early twentieth-century Britain, and they fought to get women the right to vote.

You may not agree with some of the activities these individuals used in their fight for justice, but that is not the point I am trying to make here. What I want to hopefully inspire you with is the underlying beliefs that all of these people must have had the belief that led to those actions, and the historic results they went on to achieve. Those beliefs had to have included at least a little faith, as well as a conviction, that situations and people that treated them unfairly could not and would not limit them indefinitely.

That is where I'd love you to get to, because as the saying goes: where there is a will, there is a way. I believe that the remaining two F words in the Triple F Formula will help you find the way that works for you to break free of limits that unfair situations attempt to place on you.

## Forgive

The second F word in my Triple F Formula is **Forgive**. When someone wrongs you with their words or actions, or something else happens that's unfair, I can totally relate to how painful this can be. However, it's of paramount importance that you forgive as soon as possible if there's a particular person, group of people or institution that has harmed you. This step is critical, as this will enable you to reclaim your power and keep moving towards your vision and purpose. Even if they never apologise, or they don't deserve your forgiveness, it's important that you forgive. It benefits you more than them – trust me.

I also think it is worth clarifying what I mean by forgiveness, starting with outlining what I don't mean. When I say forgive, I don't mean simply rolling over to take unacceptable behaviour or words, such as racism or sexism. By all means, please report and confront inappropriate behaviour in the right manner so that it can be dealt with through whatever justice or other systems make sense.

I also don't mean that you need to become best friends with the person or people you are forgiving. I like to say that forgiveness is free, but trust is earned. If someone loses my trust due to their actions, I completely forgive them, but they would need to earn my trust back. Depending on the situation, there may never be an opportunity for that if I conclude that certain boundaries are needed to protect myself, my energy, or my family.

What I do mean by forgiveness is to release all expectations – for example, of an apology – and let go of all negative feelings and emotions you may be harbouring towards the person or situation that wronged you. Many people feel a sense of anger when holding onto unforgiveness, and according to Johns Hopkins Medicine: 'Chronic anger puts you into a fight-or-flight mode, which results in numerous changes in heart rate, blood pressure and immune response. Those changes, then, increase the risk of depression, heart disease and diabetes, among other conditions. Forgiveness, however, calms stress levels, leading to improved health.'[1]

In their article titled 'Forgiveness: Your Health Depends on it', Johns Hopkins Medicine also stated that, 'Studies have found that the act of forgiveness can reap huge rewards for your health, lowering the risk of heart attack; improving cholesterol levels and sleep; and reducing pain, blood pressure, and levels of anxiety, depression and stress.' From my personal experience, I know that when I carry hurt, anger or resentment based on what others have done or said, that's all I can focus on a lot of the time, which blocks my ability to see and create new opportunities from the endless possibilities available to

---

[1] John Hopkins Medicine, Forgiveness: Your Health Depends On It. https://www.hopkinsmedicine.org/health/wellness-and-prevention/forgiveness-your-health-depends-on-it#:~:text=Chronic%20anger%20puts%20you%20into,levels%2C%20leading%20to%20improved%20health.

me beyond these peanuts. All this ends up keeping me stuck, wasting my time and life in a negative head space, while the people I am angry at are off living their life, not even aware of all the craziness I am dealing with between my ears. It makes no sense when you think about it like that, right? So, please give yourself the gift of forgiving others when they wrong you, whether they apologise or not.

## Focus

Once you have done this, you are ready for the final F word in the Triple F Formula, which is *Focus*. By this I mean be deliberate about what, who and where you focus. When people have hurt me in the past, I have wasted a lot of time focusing on and thinking through pointless questions like 'How could they do that?' or, 'How could they say that?' Then I have found great satisfaction in finding others who had been through the same thing and wasted even more time discussing and complaining about such pointless things. As the saying goes: misery loves company.

What I have found through my own experiences and from coaching my clients is that choosing this focus, which is the natural default reaction, is the equivalent of allowing the person who wronged us to continue to kick us repeatedly while we are still down from the initial blow. The truth is that this sort of focus can keep you stuck indefinitely. I'm so tired of seeing mums get robbed of what's possible for them, so if you're dealing with this, I strongly encourage you to take back your power and your future. You can do this by making a powerful and deliberate choice to switch your focus to making the injustice you have faced pay you back if possible. I love payback from all my problems, and you will too, the more you do this.

In case you are wondering what exactly to focus on, I suggest that you consider the familiar saying: everything happens for a reason. I have found that there is so much truth in this.

Many of us can look back at situations in the past that felt terrible at the time of going through them, but with hindsight we can see that it was a blessing in disguise. Maybe you were devastated when you weren't successful in getting a job you thought you really wanted, only to get one that was a far better fit for you afterwards. The initial failure happened for a reason.

Whatever unfair situation you are facing right now, I'd love for you to forfeit the need for hindsight and in this third step of the formula tap into that powerful wisdom within you to proactively look for the reason that may exist in the injustice you have faced.

A great way to approach this is to sit with your journal, ask yourself some great questions, and write whatever comes up. Some journaling questions and prompts I have found useful when implementing the Triple F Formula include:

1. How can I be better as a result of this?
2. If I could create anything from this situation, what would it be?
3. How can I help myself and others avoid such pain in the future?
4. I'm glad this happened because...

This is definitely not an exhaustive list of questions and prompts that you could use, but hopefully it gives you some ideas on how to deliberately choose a focus that will benefit you, and potentially others. It's important that you do this when you have definitely let go of all the negativity in the Forgive step of the formula and are hopefully feeling empowered. This is a powerful practice that can help you unlock another layer of purpose and passion that will fulfil and reward you in such a way that you might one day surprisingly feel gratitude for the unjust experience that you faced, as awful as it was.

That is exactly what happened after I suffered that discrimination at work, because it eventually led to unlocking my greater purpose of starting a business that would go on to impact lives all over the world. It is also how I can now feel deep gratitude for how unfair the motherhood experience can often be when compared to fatherhood, with the physical impacts and career penalties that so many women experience. When I was crying on my bathroom floor, feeling so lost and hard done by after having my daughter, it was shifting my focus that helped me through it. I went from thinking how unfair things can be for me, you and other women around the world, to entertaining more empowering thoughts and questions like, 'How can I help myself and others avoid such pain in the future?', and began to make empowered, destiny-altering decisions that have positively impacted me and then thousands of other women around the world.

I worked with a lovely Europe-based client, a black mother with two beautiful children. Prior to working with me, she was one of the millions around the world enraged at the years of racial injustice that George Floyd's murder in May 2020 brought to the forefront of the collective global conscience. For her personally, it was extremely difficult to witness what some black children in her country have to endure in schools and elsewhere. She was angry, tired and uninspired by negative conversations that wasted her time and left her feeling even more hopeless and powerless. Due to family and other responsibilities, she had slowed down her career significantly for the almost five years prior, and was therefore very doubtful about the difference she would be able to make. In our work together, I took her through the principles I have been sharing with you so far, including the Triple F Formula. It helped her confidence to skyrocket, and enabled her to transform her pain into power – and ultimately purpose. When I invited her to shift her focus to find the reason, she went on to envision and then create a new diversity consultancy business that is focused on being part of the solution to racial injustice in her country's school system.

Her incredible work, which includes radical improvements to school curriculums and delivering powerful workshops that foster more tolerance and inclusion, caught the attention of members of the government who value and seek her advice, and are excited to collaborate with her to create a fair future for kids in schools around the country. Her passion and her skill for getting results led to her being invited to campaign for election in local government. Less than two years after we started our work together, much to her shock and surprise, she was successfully elected, and she has now begun the work of positively impacting the lives of tens of thousands of people in her vicinity. In a few short months, she achieved what takes others many years – even decades – to accomplish, because she used the Triple F Formula to transform an unfair situation into a catapult towards destiny for herself and thousands of others.

I am so proud and blown away by her results, as is she. She told me that one of the things that made her most proud was the knowledge that her work was meaningfully and positively impacting both her own children and others in the country where she lives.

I was so moved to hear this, because I know that was the reason behind her starting her work: to fight for the best possible future for her kids. Now, from what I can see, not even the sky could limit those precious children. I'm genuinely excited to watch who they become as a result of their mum making a firm decision to have it all, and investing time to do the necessary, and at times painful, work. That is how powerful this can be in your life too, Mama. It's possible, and quite probable, that your greatest purpose will be birthed out of some of your greatest pain. So, I encourage you to remember this on the journey to your version of 'having it all'. Unfortunately, people and their biases, and the unfair situations that stem from them, may cause you pain. Rather than wasting time being angry and basically inviting them to kick you repeatedly while you are down, think of them as 'destiny helpers' that point you towards a greater destiny and purpose than you may have been planning. Invest time in implementing my Triple F Formula to carry on towards, and perhaps radically upgrade your destination of 'so much more'. Everything happens for a reason. Don't give your time, power and future to people and situations that treat you unfairly. Have faith, forgive quickly and focus on your purpose. You've got this!

## Key takeaways

- Life can be so hard and unfair at times due to no fault of our own, when people and situations seem to throw a spanner in the works of our progress.
- Depending on the particular situation and how devastating its effect, if we don't deal with it in an empowered way it can

rob us of so much time and ultimately hold us back from our destiny.

- Unfair situations can often deliver a double blow because they not only waste our time by slowing progress to our goals, how we respond or react to them can further exacerbate matters.

- People's actions and other unfair situations may make you a victim, but whether or not you stay a victim indefinitely is your choice, and in your power to control.

- To avoid staying a victim, invest time to implement my spirit- and soul-nurturing Triple F Formula, which will empower you to transform whatever pain the unfair situation caused into purpose that radically transforms your life, and the lives of others.

- The first F word in the formula is **Faith;** have faith that if people ever try to discriminate against you, or if you face other unfair situations, they cannot and will not succeed in holding you back from your destiny if you refuse to let them.

- The second F word is *Forgive;* whether they apologise or not, forgive them for you, your health and your future.

- The final F word in the formula is **Focus;** be deliberate about what, who and where you focus on. If possible, switch your focus to make the injustice you have faced pay you back.

- This powerful practice can help you unlock another layer of purpose and passion that has the power to fulfil and reward you significantly.

# Chapter 8: Guilt and Overwhelm

The dream killer of guilt and overwhelm is prolific and widespread, particularly among women and mothers – so much so that there is even a label of Mum guilt. I don't think there is a single mother that I have ever worked with, anywhere in the world, who hasn't struggled with this at some level, as they consider their to-do lists and all the necessary trade-offs that have to be made. With so many urgent and important demands on us and our time, something has to give. But what, we wonder? How can we be sure that we are making the right trade-offs? Many of us suffer serious FOMO when we pick one activity over another, so we waste time worrying long before and well after the trade-off has been made.

When inundated with meetings and invitations, we feel obliged to accept them all and be everywhere in case we miss something important, even when it doesn't make sense for us and our families. So many of us go through life making our choices and trade-offs, then worrying whether we made the right decision. This often then leads to us being elsewhere mentally, and results in even more time wasted due to our split focus and the impact of that on our effectiveness in the present. We worry that the choice to do some work-related thing instead of the thing with our kids that's happening at the same time may end up having some terrible impact on our children later on down the line; or if we do the family thing, we worry that our work performance is being judged negatively because we also have these care-giving responsibilities.

So we make choices the best way we know how, and we suffer the consequences. The result is that we end up feeling like we are failing at work, at home and everywhere – so we spend even more time feeling terrible and worrying about that. This dream killer then robs us of so much and increases the motherhood penalty we pay when we get to this point, because these feelings of failure can knock our confidence in ourselves and our work. At this point, we are less likely to go for a raise, promotion or new opportunities, even when we are capable of succeeding with them and they are well deserved. This is because of a tendency I have noticed in myself and so many women over my years of coaching, of focusing on the few areas for improvement that we notice, or that get highlighted to us in things like performance reviews, rather than celebrating the many things we are doing incredibly well.

This dream killer is equally devastating in our home lives as mothers. Many of us have at some point felt we have had no choice but to focus more on home life due to caring and other responsibilities. This can sometimes lead to us feeling unfulfilled, even resentful, because of the ambition within us to be achieving more out in the world, especially when we see friends and colleagues continuing to progress while it feels like we've been shelved. This time-consuming and exhausting mental tug of war caused by guilt, and the subsequent worry around trade-offs that we have and are yet to make, compounds the exhaustion, frustration and overwhelm that so many women around the world feel. This then makes it challenging for us to prioritise much-needed 'me time' – rest and self-care both on and offline. We feel obliged to struggle to keep up and make up for missing out on the thing we didn't choose in the moment of trade-off.

The strategies I have shared with you so far in this book for tackling the other dream killers will certainly help to reduce the instances when you will struggle with guilt and overwhelm, in particular by creating your weekly success schedule and deliberately designing a supportive personal board of directors. Even if you put together the perfect schedule and the perfect personal board of directors, if such things exist, and implement all I have shared perfectly (which is an impossible task for anyone, including me – we're only human), you will still discover there is no one-size-fits-all formula to having it all. We each have a very personal journey and purpose to walk through. Life in its unpredictability can also sneak up on you and unleash brutal circumstances that take you from having it all to losing it all in record time. Though we face many similar challenges as women and parents, the truth is that we are all so different, and there are some challenges that will be unique to us in that moment. Even for the challenges that are common to a lot of mothers, we may personally experience and perceive them very differently to another mum, depending on who we are uniquely at our core – at our soul and spirit levels.

We have different life experiences, backgrounds, dreams, motivations, levels of ambition, purpose and so much else in life that makes each one of us unique. I like to think that we are all spiritual beings, on our individual soul's journeys in these earthly bodies. For that reason, what I find deeply fulfilling, or what I find is the right choice for me in a particular situation, may be anything but that for you, and vice versa. That is why this issue of handling trade-offs has been such a difficult one for what seems like forever.

## My experience of this dream killer

As I continued to live out the purpose that my pain had led me to, I often found myself overwhelmed, but in a phenomenal way; overwhelmed with gratitude at how incredible my life had become. I was consistently able to use what came naturally to me to build a team that impacted thousands of people all over the world with our professional speaking, writing, training and executive coaching services. The sense of joy that came with this was extremely fulfilling, and the icing on the cake was the record-breaking year-on-year revenue growth we achieved. All the while, my little family was happier than ever. Our daughter was thriving at nursery, our marriage was going brilliantly, and we were excitedly expecting baby number two – a little boy! I was so relieved when we discovered the gender, because my then-three-year-old daughter had made it quite clear she would only accept a baby brother. I'm not sure what she planned to do if we brought a baby sister home, but at that twenty-week ultrasound, my husband and I laughed out loud with relief that we wouldn't have to find out. We were also filled with joy and gratitude that everything looked fine with the precious little baby we couldn't wait to hold in our arms. We had experienced a devastating loss through the miscarriage of my first pregnancy at a similar scan a few years back, so this little heart beating perfectly was one of the most beautiful things to behold and listen to. My eyes filled with happy tears as I lay there, watching. I felt like I finally had it all; I had everything I'd ever wanted. I was finally really living the dream.

Unbeknownst to me, the life of my dreams would soon become the life of my worst nightmares. Without warning, I went from having it all to losing it all due to circumstances totally out of my control. It all began a few short months after that joyous ultrasound moment, on 30 July 2019, when I went into hospital to deliver my precious boy. As I shared with you at the beginning of this book, I almost didn't survive the delivery process. I then found myself fighting for my life again less than two weeks later at home. I had planned to return to work about four to six months after he was born, as that is when I had felt ready to go back after giving birth to my daughter, but those months following my near-death experience went by in a depression-filled blur of numerous hospital appointments for both me and my son. I battled overwhelm constantly, as I continually had to deal with things that were out of my control, both in terms of my health and in my business. I couldn't seem to find the rhythm I'd expected to return to with work after my son was born. My mind was constantly racked with guilt and worry about my daughter and how she was being impacted by all this. I couldn't shake the thought that her world had been turned upside down, and I was failing her by not being as available as I would have liked to be, no matter how hard I tried.

Just when I thought things couldn't get any worse, they did, in catastrophic fashion. The Covid-19 virus emerged, causing millions of deaths around the world – it was beyond terrifying. As the world began to lock down to contain the spread of the virus, it felt like another brutal blow to my own already-crumbling personal world. From one day to the next, hundreds of thousands of dollars' worth of business that my company was almost certain we would win disappeared from our pipeline, as clients cancelled contracts and events that we would normally fly out to work on, speak at and deliver. I was relying on those funds for several different things, including paying the team and continuing with other important projects that we were working on. I had existing clients to support who were in panic mode, as the unprecedented times wreaked havoc in their lives as well. While still reeling from those shocks to the system, I discovered that, in addition to having to look after my then-eight-month-old son, who was still in need of a lot of medical attention, we would also have to homeschool our daughter, as schools were closing until further notice. The nation went into full lockdown mode, and I went from having a relatively peaceful set-up, working at home alone, to suddenly having to contend with the presence of my family at home each day.

As I tried to make sure we would have enough food for all the additional meals needed at home, I was hit with another crisis: I had clearly missed some sort of memo that everyone else seemed to have received that it was time to panic-buy food and toilet paper to survive Armageddon, and as a result we were met with empty, ransacked shelves at the supermarket. To say I was on the verge of a mental breakdown would be putting it mildly. Taking my one allocated exercise trip outdoors each day to try to calm and clear my head brought little respite. The fresh air somehow felt suffocating, even oppressive. I constantly felt claustrophobic, terrified and on edge, both inside and outdoors. There was so much to take care of that I literally had no clue what to do, never mind what I needed to do first.

*Do I focus on avoiding financial ruin by trying to fill that huge hole that has appeared in our company revenue? How on earth do I tell my team what's going on? Where can I possibly find toilet paper? We have just three rolls left! What are we supposed to be doing with homeschooling again? How do I make sure that my elderly parents are okay? How can I protect my family from this virus? Am I okay? I still feel a little weak, and not fully recovered, health-wise, does that make me more susceptible to the virus? What about my son? Will he be okay throughout all this when we can't have all the normal health visits he needs at this age? How do I help my clients who are going through their own versions of hell right now? Are we even going to get through this? This is crazy!*

Literally all day long I was bombarded by important thoughts, demands and questions that flew through my mind at breakneck speed, often in quick succession. All this left me feeling so worried and overwhelmed that after somehow making it through each day, I would lie awake at night for hours on end, full of guilt, worry and stress that I had made the wrong choices, before I finally escaped into a few hours of sleep.

Then I would wake up each morning and find myself sobbing when I remembered the nightmare life I had woken up into in this uncertain new world. I was in such a dark place mentally that often during those waking hours I wondered whether it would have been better if I had died after delivering my son. Maybe life really wasn't worth fighting for that day. This was too much for me, and I felt as though I was no good to anyone. On a few occasions, I can recall my husband tapping me on the shoulder, bringing me back down to earth after I had been staring hopelessly at a blank wall for an unknown amount of time. I had been lost in my own world, riddled with guilt, totally overwhelmed, and not really sure what to do.

After many painful weeks of existing like this, I finally had a welcome moment of clarity; a eureka moment of sorts. I realised that although this was the worst I could ever remember my life being, the circumstances and consequences I was dealing with were still minuscule compared to the infinite possibilities that had to exist beyond all this. Although I felt like I was in a mental prison every waking moment, there had to be a way out – there just had to be! If my life has taught me anything, it's that there is always a way out, no matter what it looks like, and I don't have to be a victim of my circumstances. In that very same moment, while still feeling scared, exhausted and unsure of what I would actually do, I made a firm decision. I decided that enough was enough of being crippled by depression and barely surviving in reaction mode to my overwhelming life; enough of feeling guilt and worry that almost every decision I made was the wrong one for my family, myself and my business. I decided that something had to change, and fast!

I had been regularly accessing and leveraging my internal wisdom to help me prioritise conflicting responsibilities for a long time. I had even become good at navigating crisis situations with the six-step CRISIS success plan I mentioned earlier. But when this back-to-back series of crises hit me unexpectedly, I got totally derailed, and my regular practice of continuously tapping into my spirit for insight was long forgotten. It was very apparent that I had disconnected from the power available within me, given how stuck I felt. I therefore resolved that it was time to start again. I decided to begin by checking in about what the most important things were that I needed to focus on, both professionally and personally. As I listened in for that intuition, I heard: 'Lose weight and start a membership programme.' *What?* It didn't make any sense to me, as I was sure it would be something to do with my kids. I was feeling like the worst mum ever, due to how scattered and lost I felt; I constantly felt like I was failing them. So I kept checking again and again, and got the same divine guidance from within me: 'Lose weight and start a membership programme.'

I knew from prior experience that the guidance I receive when accessing wisdom from within can sometimes make no sense whatsoever to my logical mind, but I had also repeatedly seen the ways in which this guidance seems to miraculously factor in things I have no conscious knowledge of in the moment when I check in. By that point in 2020, I'd learnt to trust and get on with following even the most bizarre guidance, knowing that all would be revealed at the right time.

I thought through the instructions again, and to be honest I initially felt even more overwhelmed and exhausted. I was not even sure I knew what a membership programme was, never mind how to start one. I had also tried unsuccessfully to lose my excess baby weight before, many times. How was I supposed to succeed now with all this chaos happening in the world as well? Thankfully, the beautiful thing about checking in for divine guidance is you can keep accessing it to get the different pieces of the puzzle. So I got up early the next day while the family were all still asleep to tap into my spirit for more answers. I started with the weight loss, as I sensed that that was the priority. I checked in and asked, 'How am I supposed to do this with everything else that's going on? I don't even know what I am doing with this! God knows I have tried during more normal days and failed miserably. What chance do I have now when I feel like my whole world is literally falling apart?' Deep within my spirit I heard, 'It's not that dramatic, Maxine. All it takes is a little bit of exercise regularly, and a healthy diet. You just need some guidance on how to do this and help to stay motivated.' That sounded simple enough, but how on earth was I supposed to find that in the midst of a global pandemic?

I sensed that the best thing I could do in that moment was to wait, as things would become clear soon. That very same day, I received an unusual email from the fitness company I had purchased one of the many ununsed workout DVD sets from; bought with good intentions but then somehow never followed through with. The email asked, 'Do you have 10–30 pounds to lose, very little time to work out, and need a bit of a push?' They were running a study group kicking off in the next few days and needed participants who would be willing to use their programme by completing the short, effective workouts through the day, and following meal guidance with the help of a dedicated sports nutritionist. My jaw hit the floor. This was before I even reached the best part. All this was also part of a competition: the most impressive weight-loss transformations would be in with a chance of receiving an all-expenses paid trip to Miami for a glamorous photo shoot and much more!

I couldn't believe it, this was everything I knew I needed! I love competition – few things motivate me like a bit of healthy competition, usually against myself to beat my last result. The chance to do this with a group and to be kept accountable every step of the way was incredible. I signed up immediately, and with their guidance I discovered the healthy foods I could buy and prepare quickly and easily, even with all the madness still going on with panic buying in the supermarkets. Through the daily coaching and support I received as part of the study, and continuing to tap into my spirit for guidance, I also managed to prioritise the 15–30 minute blocks of time I needed to work out most days of the week.

It gradually went from excruciating to challenging, to bearable, to finally becoming enjoyable! I started to crave the endorphin hit I would get from my workouts as they somehow energised me and gave me powerful mental clarity that helped me tackle the rest of my tasks for home and work with greater efficiency and effectiveness. This included being the more loving, present and supportive wife and mum I want to be, and researching how to go about building an impactful membership programme in my working life.

I kept tapping into my spirit for guidance every morning, and throughout the day, about what I needed to be focused on, and what my daily must-do items were. There were always fewer items than I expected on the list, and completing this was always manageable in the time I had. Best of all, I was able to focus on the must-do items and confidently ignore what was left with little to no guilt for my choices. I could finally switch off from work without guilt and worry each day. It was so freeing to be reminded that just because something had to be done, it didn't have to be done by me, right at this moment.

I got more confident focusing on just prioritising the must-do items each day when I noticed that, day after day, the world did not end when I left certain things undone. The numerous things that I had been feeling pressured to that did not make the list each day were deleted, delegated or done at the time my spirit suggested – it began to work like clockwork. I was guided by my spirit to get the support of a highly skilled therapist and life coach who helped me to work through the depression and other mental challenges I had been struggling with. Getting this help was a powerful and life-changing experience that I highly recommend to anyone struggling with their mental health.

I was also led to seek out an incredible parenting coach who taught me how to ensure that each of my children got what they needed from me, beyond their basic needs, so that they felt safe, secure, significant and loved. It was so wonderful to be able to invest that time in them, and then face the other challenges in my life and business with full confidence and zero guilt about how I was parenting. As I worked with my parenting coach, I marvelled at how things had been transformed – before that moment of clarity began to change everything, I was often motivated by guilt; I would lay aside other pressing responsibilities to spend time with my kids, then be emotionally unavailable to them throughout our time together. My mind would be elsewhere, often entertaining overwhelming, depressing or morbid thoughts. I could now see that this was not helpful for them or me. My kids didn't need a guilt-ridden, scatter-brained mum who was barely present, but there was no way I could have figured that out in the mental state I was in. I just kept making knee-jerk reactions to the feelings of guilt, which made matters worse. I am so thankful that I found a way to break that cycle, and to start putting on my own oxygen mask first, again by getting help for both my physical and mental health.

That got me to the point where I am now – a place where I no longer hold myself to impossible standards of perfection. Instead of being motivated by guilt, I started being led by love, as I implemented proven parenting strategies that help me discern and provide what my children need as best as I can. My relationships with my family were radically transformed. In fact, by less than six months in, just before my fortieth birthday, this simple switch of being powerfully guided by my spirit had pretty much transformed my whole life. Eating healthily and exercising regularly had become firmly instilled habits, as routine to me as waking up and brushing my teeth – I find it hard to miss a day. I ended up being celebrated as one of the top transformations of the fitness study group, and being used as a powerful testimonial that hopefully helps the company make a lot more sales, though the Miami trip for winners was no longer an option due to Covid travel restrictions. I lost over ten kilograms and went from looking like I was still pregnant with my son when I started to actually being able to see my abs for the first time in my life! I honestly didn't think any abs existed under the belly fat that had been with me for decades – I was genuinely shocked to see them emerge after having two kids!

According to my fitness stats, I had the body of a twenty-four-year-old at forty, and I somehow managed to start looking way better than I did in my twenties. My mind was blown with how unrecognisable I was once again – but for the right reasons this time. The best part of all this had very little to do with my appearance, though. I was most grateful for the change that all this enabled in my relationships, health and business. This healthy lifestyle was conducive to my energy and creative ideas skyrocketing. I went on to pivot my business and launch the new membership programme. I had incredible women from five continents sign up to benefit from access to me, my expertise and each other to take action and be kept accountable to working towards their incredible visions.

As things got worse and worse with the pandemic, my programme was a safe place where women could come together and realise that they were not alone, and to get the necessary support to make a masterpiece of whatever raw hand life had dealt them.

I have lost count of how many times I was moved to happy tears upon reading their numerous testimonials on how being part of this incredible, loving and supportive community positively impacted their lives, families and careers. It was such a fulfilling experience to be part of helping us all thrive, rather than settling for barely surviving during those challenging times. I dread to think what would have happened to these amazing women, their families and their communities if I had not invested the necessary time to get myself back on track to find my purpose when faced with the guilt and overwhelm that was brought on by great turbulence and uncertainty around me.

The pandemic and other challenges that 2020 threw at us as women added several more layers to the already complicated juggling act that we had been dealing with, stretching us to our very limits. One study calculated that the value of unpaid care work performed by women in the wake of the pandemic was the equivalent of ten trillion dollars, or thirteen per cent of global GDP. A good chunk of that staggering amount of work was done by many women who were also responsible for delivering an incredible amount of value in the workplace. Needless to say, there were conflicts and clashes, often many times a day, between our professional and personal lives, which many of us didn't unfortunately have an effective method for tackling.

The default response from most women I have come across in my life and work is to get into reaction mode when crises hit, making knee-jerk reactions to whatever comes up, then dealing with the adverse consequences. Even those of us who have been regularly checking in for intuition on how to create and live a fulfilling life are tempted to fall back into reaction mode when life gets overwhelming. Other times, when our intuition has led us to a period of success and fulfilment in life, we get busy living the dream, and we feel we no longer have time to keep checking in. These are all big mistakes. Walking through life without the regular practice of checking in with ourselves will eventually lead us into cycles of guilt, worry and overwhelm. It will also likely lead us to experience that nagging voice that pops up from time to time in the back of our minds to tell us that we are off-track from where we are meant to be in life – usually because we are.

There is a much better way. While there may not be a one-size-fits-all solution to our various challenges as mums, this final strategy will help us all to more confidently make our trade-offs, navigate our unique paths, and overcome guilt and overwhelm in our lives. It involves making it a non-negotiable priority each day, no matter what else is going on, to tap into that internal wisdom we have been talking about throughout this journey together. It will help you navigate whatever circumstances you are facing until you are back on track to the right definition of having it all for you, in your current season of life.

In my opinion, we are never too busy, overwhelmed, or anything else to do this. If you are drowning in to-dos and trade-offs you have to make and are wondering where to start, your absolute first priority should be to tune in to that wisdom. Doing this will allow you to access and leverage what I like to call your spirit power to tackle the issues you're facing more confidently, without wasting time in guilt, overwhelm and worry. Mine and my clients' experience has been that even when our logical minds lack clarity on what the right choice to make is in any given situation, when we tune in for that guidance, our spirit somehow knows the right thing for us to do, that is right for us personally – every single time. Through our experiences, I have found that the reason most women's to-do lists are so overwhelming, guilt- and worry-inducing is because these lists are full of things that have nothing to do with their purpose. When we live like this, we waste and spend time in reaction mode, working frantically on all these things that have nothing to do with our individual soul's journey. It's no wonder we end up feeling stressed, unfulfilled and like we are not where we are meant to be in life. Making it non-negotiable to consistently access powerful guidance from our spirit helps us to separate the urgent to-dos that can keep us in the default reaction mode, from the important to-dos that empower us to make the right personal choices for our purpose and families. As we make these right choices consistently, we continue in creation mode even when faced with unprecedented challenges and uncertain times.

When I introduce women to this way of living, the main concern I hear from them is over whether by living this way they'll still manage to get everything done. The honest answer is, absolutely not. There are many things that you will not end up doing, but I also think it's worth considering whether that really matters in the grand scheme of things. The answer to that is also absolutely not.

So many of us have bought the lie that we need to be some sort of superwoman who does everything, and wears being busy as a badge of honour in order to be seen as successful and having it all. The truth is, that's not real success for many women, and it's simply not possible to do it all if we want to avoid burnout. It's not your purpose to live a life busy and crushed by the weight of expectations that have nothing to do with the beautiful journey and purpose your soul is here for.

## The SPIRIT Power Process

The beautiful news is that we were never meant to do it all. We simply can't if we want to *have* it all. And as I said before, by having it all, I mean having all that we are meant to have in this season of life, according to our soul's purpose and journey, which looks very different from one woman to the next. To find your unique path, regularly tap into your spirit for guidance on how to reach your current vision of having it all, and start stepping into it as you are guided. As you do this, you will find that you have all you are meant to have in each stage of your life, and it will be fulfilling.

You can do this by utilising my six-step SPIRIT Power Process. SPIRIT is an acronym that I hope helps make this easy for you to remember and follow.

## S: Set aside time

The S in SPIRIT stands for *Set aside time* – utilise this time to tap into your spirit and access your precious internal wisdom. Specifically carving out time for this needs to be a step all on its own, because it does not happen automatically for most of us. It's important to set aside a time to get this guidance in order to help you prioritise and confidently choose between trade-offs. There are some circumstances where you may need to make a trade-off unexpectedly during the day; in which case, be sure to set aside time right there and then to work through the rest of the steps rather than just reacting. For normal day-to-day life, though, it is a powerful practice to set aside a regular time to do this when creating your weekly success schedule as I guided you to in Chapter 1. I personally prefer doing this early in the morning before everyone else in the family gets up, and before checking email, social media or anything else, so that I get my purpose-driven to-dos down before all the external things vying for my attention and reaction can influence my thinking. Early morning may or may not work for you, and that's okay – the key is to decide when does, then show up for yourself, just as you do for all the other important people in your life.

## P: Prepare to receive

The next step in the SPIRIT Power Process is P, which stands for **Prepare to receive**. Preparation is crucial because, as you may recall, over ninety-nine per cent of who we are is invisible energy, so the state we are in energetically, in terms of our mind, will and emotions can greatly affect our ability to hear and receive guidance.

Think about a moment when you were distracted by or worried about something. If someone came to tell you something else in that moment, chances are you would miss some, if not most, of what they had to say. I know I can't be the only one who has had a loved one ask me something along the lines of, 'Don't you remember when I told you about this?' It can be the same with accessing your spirit for guidance, so you want to prepare by limiting distractions or anything else that could affect your ability to hear clearly. This can include things like finding a quiet place to go to and clearing all distractions from your mind so you can focus. I have found getting a piece of paper and basically doing a brain dump of all the random things going through my mind to be pretty effective for this. You may find that when you start trying to do this thoughts like, *I must remember to add milk to the shopping list,* or an annoying thing that someone did or said start coming to mind. Write it all down so I get it out of my head. One of my clients remarked on how therapeutic this brain dump is for her, as she treats it like a place where she can vent and rant about things that are upsetting to her that her husband and others may not understand. After the brain dump she feels seen and heard, which then frees her mind and emotions to get guidance on the way forward.

If this idea resonates with you, try it and see how it works for you. One final thing that I have found to be extremely powerful preparation after my brain dump is to practise gratitude by writing down at least five things I am profoundly grateful for. Even if I start this process worried or fearful, focusing on what I'm grateful for always helps get me into an optimistic emotional state, which is very conducive to getting invaluable internal insights into my experience.

## I: Inquire of your intuition

Once you have prepared yourself to receive, the next step in the process is I, which stands for *Inquire of your intuition*. There are numerous ways to do this, as we have been discussing, and as many of us mums are naturally intuitive, you may already have one that works for you. If so, I encourage you to keep using what works to get direction on the best way forward with the choices or trade-offs you have to make in your set-aside or more spontaneous moments. Every time you are faced with a trade-off between your personal and professional life, rather than choosing the default of perhaps automatically picking work because you're worried about how your colleagues or boss would perceive your choice, or automatically picking family because you feel guilty if you don't, take a moment to use your tried-and-tested method to inquire of your intuition what the right choice is for you and your individual soul's purpose and journey in this moment.

If you are new to this process, I recommend you get started using the method I have already shared with you – simply ask yourself really great questions. To recap, by great questions I mean those that you actually need or want to know the answer to. For example, if you have a work presentation that clashes with an event at your child's school, a great question to ask to receive intuitive guidance could be, 'Where do I need to be today to be living fully in my purpose?'

A not-so-great question that I have found myself and others asking in similar situations is, 'Why does this keep happening to me?' This question is usually accompanied by feelings of frustration, hopelessness and overwhelm. The answer to this latter question in my case was usually, 'It keeps happening because your kids are really young, and you are therefore in a season of life where you have many conflicting responsibilities.' This was not the answer I needed, and it definitely didn't move me towards my vision; rather, it increased the amount of time I spent feeling frustrated, hopeless, overwhelmed and, of course, guilty when I chose work. Be sure to ask great questions in this step.

In terms of the practicality of using great questions to hear from your intuition, I recommend using trial and error, if necessary, to find what works for you. I personally like to do this exercise in my journal by writing out the question, listening for a moment before starting to write, without overthinking or trying to force it, then I watch to see what comes up. There is usually a strong knowing within me when I have stumbled upon the right answer as I write. I have advised clients to make choices in this way, and many have been surprised that their intuition led them to the family event when they would have automatically chosen work, and vice versa. As they followed the rest of the steps in the process, they were even more surprised and delighted that there was no major catastrophe, as they had feared in the past. Best of all, they felt zero guilt and worry when they were at the personal or work thing, because they knew they were exactly where their soul needed to be in that moment to stay on purpose and on track.

## R: Resolve to trust and obey

When you have your intuitive guidance and you know in your gut exactly what choice or trade-off you are meant to make, you are ready for the next step, R, which stands for **Resolve to trust and obey**. This step is key because, as I alluded earlier, the answer you get may not make sense to your logical mind. Our intuition mysteriously factors in aspects of our future that we may not even be aware of yet. I remember thinking 'lose weight' was such a bizarre and ridiculous suggestion from my intuition, given all the chaos that was going on in my life when I did this process at the start of the pandemic. As I shared, little did I know how much the healthier lifestyle would positively impact pretty much every area of my life, even business marketing! So many women who, like me, had been struggling to lose weight for so long were attracted to work with me due to seeing that transformation and wondering how they could do it too. There is no way my logical mind could have seen and strategised that – not in a million years. I was in such fear and panic that, to my logical mind, the priority was finding toilet paper. So, I invite you to resolve to trust and obey even the most bizarre directions from your intuition.

One final point of caution in this step: resist the urge to compare the guidance you receive to what your family, friends or anyone else would offer. I'm not proposing that you blindly follow any illegal or wrong suggestions that others would advise against here; true intuitive guidance would not suggest you act in a way that is harmful to you or anyone else.

What I am advising against is comparing the guidance you receive to what is 'normal' or 'good' advice in your family, culture or anything else. When I received the guidance to start a membership programme and fully understood what that was, I felt that the suggestion to start one was terrible advice to the logical mind, due to my business model at the time. Given the necessary pivots I would have to make in my business in the future to be able to fulfil my purpose, however, it was actually a genius suggestion, though again, one that I could never have seen and strategised in a million years at the time of making the trade-off.

The world of certainty about the way we do things that we were born into no longer exists. At the time of me writing this, things still remain uncertain and unpredictable. So in order to thrive in whatever's next, as you tap into your SPIRIT power for guidance, your intuition will very likely suggest things that you and your personal board of directors may have no frame of reference for. Resolve to trust and obey that intuitive guidance knowing that you are a unique, one-of-a-kind masterpiece; that you are on this earth at this time for a specific purpose that you and others may not fully understand until it manifests through your spirit-inspired actions.

## I: Inform those affected

As you resolve to trust and obey, and begin to take inspired action, getting more intuitive guidance along the way if needed, you will need to complete the next step: I, which is to *Inform those affected*. For example, if you are using this process to decide between a family and professional trade-off, if you are guided to choose family, then confidently and unapologetically inform those at the work-related activity that you are unavailable for the activity happening at the same time there. If it's necessary and possible, you can arrange for the work to be delayed or delegated. Many employers are very understanding of the immense pressures facing working mothers and are willing to be flexible. If that is not the case for you, get further guidance from your intuition on what to do.

You can also inquire of your intuition on the best way to inform those affected so you can do this confidently and unapologetically. As I have done this more and more, both in the past as an employee and now as a business owner, I have discovered that the overwhelming need I felt to apologise for the flexibility I required was rooted in giving way more detail than was necessary. As an employee, I wasted time worrying what my colleagues would think about me needing to miss a meeting because I had to attend something with my daughter. As I checked in to my intuition one time I got, 'Spare them the details, that's irrelevant right now, just tell them you are already booked at that time, and therefore unavailable, and suggest another way for what they need done to happen.'

As I started doing that, and either delegating the responsibility or doing it at a time when I was free, I was amazed that almost no one asked me what I was doing during the time I was booked and unavailable, as long as they got what they needed from me. Even when they did have to know why I was unavailable, they didn't mind that I was taking the well-deserved flexibility to create the harmony necessary between my personal and professional life for good mental and physical health, because I focused on always delivering what they needed done, and most of the time I overdelivered.

Likewise, if your intuition suggested that you focus on work instead of the family or personal to-dos, as mine has also done on many occasions, you need to inform those affected and check in with your intuition on what else you can do to help in your absence. I had to do this on the occasion when my son was sick and I was due to be hosting an event – I was able to call on the help of my mother to take care of my son in my absence, rather than cancelling or making my husband sacrifice his own work commitments to enable me to carry out my hosting role.

## T: Tell others on a need-to-know basis

The final step is T, which is *Tell others on a need-to-know basis*. I included this step as I learnt the hard way that not everyone needs to know what you are doing all the time, particularly in those moments when your choices are ones that you know deep in your gut are the right thing to do but that may not make full sense to your logical mind yet. Sadly, even people who you'd expect to support you may end up judging and criticising your choices, which can in turn make you more likely to start feeling guilty again and more tempted to quit. Imagine this same story about the painful choice I had to make of leaving my son to go to work after that awful night of him being sick: if I'd gone beyond telling just those affected to broadcast the situation to others who didn't really need to know, I would have opened myself up to the opinions and potential judgement of people who have no idea of the intimate details of my situation, purpose and journey.

As I have been saying, we are all called to, and fulfilled by, different things. A mum who is totally fulfilled by the incredible and challenging work of being a full-time, stay-at-home mum may hear the story of me leaving my son in the care of my mother and say something like, 'What kind of mum leaves her sick child to go to work?' Hearing such feedback would of course pile on the guilt and doubt for me, despite knowing that I was meant to be at work that day, that my son would be incredibly well taken care of, and that if I stayed home I would be miserable wondering what impact missing the event could have on my career.

The same thing would apply in reverse for the full-time stay-at-home mum who has taken the decision to leave the workforce. If she starts trying to share her choices and the reasons behind them with former classmates and colleagues who are on a totally different journey and career path, they may suggest, explicitly or implicitly, that it's a crazy idea to be a stay-at-home mum after the tens of thousands of pounds and years that she's invested in getting her education, as well as the time and experience in her career thus far. Hearing this could prompt serious feelings of worry and doubt about the decision that she knows is right for her and her family at that phase of her life.

Can you see how destructive sharing unnecessarily can be? Please do yourself a favour and only tell those who need to know; not everyone will understand and support your choices, and that's okay. We are all on our own journeys; in time you can use the SPIRIT Power Process to find people who are safe to share with, who will support and celebrate you.

That is the complete six-step SPIRIT Power Process. It might seem like a lot, but the more you do it, the more you will find you can get through the steps relatively quickly. As difficult choices and trade-offs pop up, try to default to running through this powerful process, instead of responding with a guilt- and overwhelm-motivated knee-jerk reaction. The more you do this, the quicker it will become natural for you. I promise this will be such a gamechanger in terms of helping you overcome the guilt, worry, FOMO, overwhelm and stress that we can face. It is also a powerful tool for getting you unstuck and moving along the path to success where you may have failed before.

I'm excited for you to experience this feeling of being miraculously led by your spirit to seemingly tailor-made opportunities that make the impossible possible for you. Through consistently using this process, I am back to feeling like I am doing what I was born to do for me, my family, my clients, and the world. This current definition of having it all fulfils me more than I can find the words to describe. Surprisingly, one of the best parts of all of this is that there is no fear about what I would do if I lost it all. I've been there, and done that; both through my own foolish mistakes when I was younger, and more recently through no fault of my own. I know from the process of rising from the ashes in both cases, and from helping countless women also rise from their own version of the ashes, the way out is exactly the same. No matter how we get to the low points in life, we transform them when we stop being moved by what we can see, and begin to regularly seek guidance from our spirit to tap into the infinite possibilities in the unseen realm, and pull on them till they replace the circumstances we were tired of seeing in our lives. Seeing and experiencing this over and over again has taught me there is no need to fear. There is infinite power available within me to build back way better, come what may. It's the same for you too Mama, you are that powerful.

Let me end with this quick story about overcoming Mum guilt. On my daughter's third birthday, I was dropping her off to nursery.

At that point, I had just gone into business for myself full-time and was keen to build it to replace the salary I was used to from my last employer. I had quite a lot of work to do that day, so I was keen to drop her off and get on with it. The plan was that after work and nursery we would have a small family celebration at home, then at the weekend she would have a party with her friends. All morning, my daughter was incredibly clingy, telling me that she did not want to go to nursery. I needed to get to work and had a lot to do when I got there, so I kept telling her she had to go, and practically had to drag her in, before quickly running off to the car to drive to work. As I sat in the car, the familiar wave of Mama guilt hit me. *What am I doing? How can I leave her? She was so sure she didn't want to go to nursery today. But I have to work, I have so many important deliverables, I can't just not work, right? There's no one to pay me if I don't work.*

After wasting a few minutes going back and forth through both options in my mind, I remembered to use the SPIRIT Power Process to decide what to do. I felt a strong guidance to go back into the nursery to get her. I resolved to trust and obey, I made a few calls to inform those affected, then I cleared my calendar for the day, deleting, delegating and delaying as necessary so I could take the day off. Then I went back into the nursery. As I approached, I saw the most heartbreaking picture of my Chiamaka, tears streaming down her face as she looked out of the window, refusing to be her usual happy playful self with her friends. And this was of course her birthday of all days!

I excitedly told her that I was here to take her home and do whatever she wanted to do. Her tears immediately turned to laughter, and she started jumping up and down. We went home, played games, drew pictures, did crafts and had a wonderful time. I am still not sure exactly why she didn't want to be at nursery that day – she was absolutely fine and laughing with her friends again the next day. I am also not sure why it was so important for me to honour her choice, but I know that in my gut it felt like it was the right thing to do. I could tell that the fact that I came back had a massive impact on her. This means the world to me, as research in the field of psychology has found that it is in these early years of life that our beliefs about life, our worthiness and how things work in the world are formed. These beliefs can then go on to either limit or liberate us to reach our greatness in later life.

I am hopeful that this simple choice made a positive difference in her life and future. The funny thing is, as I recall this story, I can't even remember what work it was that I was supposed to be doing that day, despite it feeling super important at the time. It probably was important, as I was in the foundation stages of building my business with a team to pay and without the luxury or privilege of investors, or anyone to ask for paid time off. As usual, my gut instincts and the spirit of my inner wisdom knew what lay ahead, and guided me to the right choice for that moment and others as I continued to check in. I closed that business year five months later with numerous delighted clients around the world, which enabled me to more than quadruple the corporate income I was worried about replacing, all while experiencing very little guilt and overwhelm in my personal life. Your spirit can also guide you to what's best for you, your family and your future, and the best path for you to have it all. Invest time daily to engage your spirit through this process and watch how you go from feeling guilt and overwhelm, to confidence and clarity as you make your choices and trade-offs.

## Key takeaways

- There are numerous conflicts and clashes, often many times a day, between our professional and personal lives that many of us don't have an effective method for tackling.
- The default is to continue reacting to what comes up and dealing with the adverse consequences. This, of course, keeps us in cycles of guilt, worry and overwhelm, with a continuous ache deep within our soul that tells us we are 'off-track' from where we are meant to be in life.
- To overcome this, use the SPIRIT Power Process to tap into your internal wisdom, if necessary, to redefine what 'having it all' means for you in this season of your life, and to then tackle trade-offs and prioritise your to-dos confidently, without wasting time in guilt and overwhelm.
- SPIRIT is an acronym:
    - The S stands for **Set aside time** to tap into your spirit for guidance. Ideally, make this a daily scheduled habit, but also be prepared to set aside time right away if unexpected choices and trade-offs pop up.
    - The next step in the SPIRIT Power Process is P, which stands for **Prepare to receive**. Doing a brain dump of distracting thoughts and practising gratitude are great ways to prepare to receive insight.
    - Once you are prepared to receive, the next step is I, which stands for **Inquire of your intuition**. Find the way that works best for you, such as using a journal, to ask great questions of yourself that lead you to the vision of clarity and confidence with your choices and trade-offs.
    - When you have your intuitive guidance and you know in

your gut exactly what choice or trade-off you are meant to make, you are ready for the next step, R, which is *Resolve to trust and obey*.

o As you resolve to trust and obey, and you begin to take those steps, getting more intuitive guidance along the way if needed, you will need to complete the next step, I, which is to *Inform those affected*.

o The final step is T, which is *Tell others on a need-to-know basis*.

# Conclusion

We started our journey together in this book with the story of my near-death experience. If I had died that morning, so much of my purpose would have been left unfulfilled. I dare not think what that would have meant for my family, friends and all the amazing women like you that I was meant to help. One sobering thought that does often occur to me, though, is the fact that that day came without warning. I went to bed the night before blissfully unaware that in a few short hours I would be fighting for my life. Ultimately, none of us really knows when we will take our last breath, so it's wise to live in a way that, if that day is today, we would die without regret, knowing we fully achieved our purpose.

As we conclude our journey together through this book, let me ask you this: if you were to die today, would you have truly lived? Would you have achieved the dream of having, experiencing and doing all you are meant to do? I want more than anything for the answer to be a resounding yes! For you, and me, when that day eventually comes.

With dream killers left unchecked in our lives, that is just a pipe dream. If you see yourself settling in any way for less than your best, most incredible life, then today is the day to start making changes – for you, your kids and so many others whose lives and breakthroughs are connected to yours. The life in which you have it all doesn't happen by chance, you need to take it by force. I believe in the masterpiece that is you. Remember, you are already worthy and important. You don't need to do anything to earn or be worthy of daily time for holistic self-care. You deserve to be brilliantly well taken care of, so you can fulfil the purpose you are here for. The powerful strategies I have shared with you will help you to do that. Revisit them as often as you need to as things come up that threaten to take you off course and make you feel like you have to settle for less than you are meant for. Regardless of what things look or feel like right now, anything is possible for you, because there are infinite possibilities in the unseen realm to connect to and to pull into the visible realm via your soul and spirit. You are powerful enough to create a life that far surpasses your wildest dreams.

I encourage you to remember that the answers you need to keep moving towards that life come from within you. Check in with yourself before reaching out to others for help and opinions. That way you will be directed to the right people, places and things that will work for you and your unique situation. Show up for yourself daily, as faithfully as you show up for others in your life, and just watch and see how dramatically different your life looks and feels in just a few short months.

I also invite you to track your progress as best you can. There's nothing like seeing how much progress you are making to keep you motivated to continue. Consider taking a snapshot of how things currently are in your journal when you are finished with this book. Paint a vivid picture of what the peanuts you hope to change look like right now. Write it all down so you have a detailed 'before' picture to track your progress against. Then look at your vision and work out where you would need to be in ninety days' time if you were on track to create that life. As you begin to tackle the dream killers that are most relevant in your life, I encourage you to track your progress from the 'before' snapshot to your ninety-day goals each week as you create your weekly success schedule.

Trust me, as you see yourself making progress and see how far you eventually go, you'll never want to come back to the life you were living when you first picked up this book. I would really love to hear how your life changes, so please connect with me on social media and via my website: www.thefutureisgreater.com. I often share free resources on both to support you on your journey to having it all, so take advantage of those to stay motivated and on track. My hope is that as you do this, like so many of my clients, your transformation is so radical that you struggle to believe you ever lived like you do now. That's exactly what it feels like when I think back over aspects of my life. I struggle to believe that was really me now that I am living the 'so much more' that I was always meant for. Mama, you too are meant for so much more, and you now have the tools to create and step into it.

Go ahead and let life get so good, so that as you transition from this earth there isn't an ounce of regret, just immense gratitude and fulfilment in knowing you gave life your best shot, for you, your family and your world. You've got this! I believe in you.

# Acknowledgments

God - it's all from You, to You and through You. Thank you for this epic adventure that is my life with You. We've been through so much, yet I feel like we're just getting started, and I'm here for ALL of it.

Nnamdi, Chiamaka, and Nnamdi Jr - my fellow Nwanerians. You are my Why, my World, My Greatest Teachers. Thank you for your love, incredible support, and for giving me purpose. You were so worth fighting for! I love you to the moon and back, and am eternally grateful for, and to you.

Mama Ye, It's very unlikely this book would exist without you. I believe the few words I was blessed to have you speak over me during your lifetime are a huge part of why I escaped an early grave on multiple occasions, and am here write these words. Words that I pray will continue your incredible legacy for generations to come. I will forever be thankful to and for you. I miss you, I love you, and I look forward to the day we will meet again.

Mum and Dad thank you for raising me the right way, and keeping the faith when it looked like I departed from it. I couldn't have achieved even a tiny fraction of what I have without your unwavering support, selfless sacrifices, and so much else you have been, and done over the years. My achievements are as much yours as mine as a reward for giving up so much for your children, and the future generations to have the opportunities we do.

To Andy, Marylee, and Uche - we are, and will always be the fantastic 4. I truly hit the jackpot when it comes to siblings. Thank you for putting up with my weird and wonderful ways over the years and always being there. This goes for all the spouses and kids we've grown into as well. I love you all so much and thank you for your support through thick and thin.

To my extended family and dear friends, you are my amazing village, and I am beyond blessed to have you. I love how I can always count on you to be there.

Queen Esther Dumelo - I'm so thankful God blessed me with a friend like you who is far more precious than jewels aged just 11! You and your amazing family have been such a blessing to me over the decades. It's so rare to have friends love you as you are, while simultaneously seeing, and pushing you towards all you can be. Thank you for seeing this book long before I did, and giving it life with your powerful words for my 40th. May your words continue to create greatness in yours and others' lives.

Nissi Sanders you have been the Coach, Spiritual Midwife, and so much more that helped keep the dream of birthing this book alive. I can say with confidence that I would not have made it this far without your support - you are truly a heaven sent gift, and I love and appreciate you so much!

Pete & Sarah Wynter, my SPH family, and all my phenomenal mentors, I thank you for all the love, support, covering, guidance, opportunities, and so much more on the journey of bringing this to life. My family and I are beyond blessed to have you in our lives.

To my incredible Clients, past and present; you inspire me so much, and my heart is full of gratitude for you. Looking back over my life as I wrote, I couldn't help but think how so much of it was preparation for us to meet and have the most impactful experience working together. You give my life so much purpose and meaning, and teach me so much. My hope is that the ripple effect of our work spreads further than any of us could dream as readers grab hold of and implement the powerful strategies your lives have proved work brilliantly. Continue to live your best lives without apology. I am so proud of you!

To all the fantastic women that took the time to have a research call with me as I wrote, thank you for your time, candid insights, suggestions and so much more. You made the writing process more enjoyable, and far less lonely than it could have been. You also helped enrich the end result.

Rose Sandy your incredible dream of the Harper Collins Academy made my dream possible of publishing this possible. The Academy was such a life and game changer for me and so many others. Our voices can now be published and read thanks to your brilliant and generous programme. Thank you for seeing "something special" in this book as you kept saying when it was just an idea, and for your brilliant "book doctoring" along the way as it came to life. I hope to make you proud, and help you feel it was all worth it to sacrifice your retirement plans by launching the Academy much earlier than planned.

To Lisa, Marleigh and all the team at HQ thank you for believing in me, giving me a chance, and for bringing this dream to life far more spectacularly I ever could have done without you. You are simply the BEST!

## ONE PLACE. MANY STORIES

Bold, innovative and
empowering publishing.

FOLLOW US ON:

@HQStories